The Little Book
of
FUNNY
QUOTATIONS

The Little Book

of

FUNNY QUOTATIONS

Edited by

ALISON BULLIVANT

Parragon
Queen Street House
4 Queen Street
Bath BA1 1HE

Special Edition for PAST TIMES®, Oxford, England, 1999

Produced by Magpie Books, an imprint of
Robinson Publishing Ltd, London

Copyright © Parragon 1998

Cover illustration courtesy of Popperfoto

ISBN 0 75252 685 5

A copy of the British Library Cataloguing-in-Publication Data
is available from the British Library

Printed in China

PAST TIMES®

Contents

Introduction

It's an odd job, making decent people laugh.

Molière

The Little Book of Funny Quotations *is compiled from the reflections of some of the most brilliant minds of the past and present. From the deeply philosophical assertions of Ambrose Bierce and Mark Twain, wrapped as they often are in a sweetener of humor, and the acidic but enviable wit of Oscar Wilde, with his outrageous and audacious statements, to the sharply observed social commentary of more modern writers like P.J. O'Rourke, Bill Bryson and Fran Lebowitz.*

There is also a delicious mix of the best of the badinage of Noël Coward, the barbed ripostes of Groucho Marx, the slightly off-the-wall and terribly English humor of P.G. Wodehouse ("Ice formed on the Butler's upper slopes"), and the dry repartee of Sir Winston Churchill, to name but a few. All have been left to posterity – what a gift!

This is a book to dip into and perhaps from which to steal a few lines to drop into conversation or to use as a deft retort when our own wit fails us. And why not? In the words of Ralph Waldo Emerson: "Next to the originator of a good sentence is the first quoter of it"; and although we won't be the first, we certainly won't be the last.

Chapter 1

THE ARTS

Shut up Arnold, or I'll direct this play the way you wrote it!

John Dexter (to Arnold Wesker)

Comments and opinions from the great names of the world of music, books, journalism, film, theater and television, from Gioacchino Rossini to George Bernard Shaw, the Arts have provided often cutting but endlessly amusing material — at least to those at which it is not directed.

Madam, you have between your legs an instrument capable of giving pleasure to thousands – and all you can do is scratch it.

> Thomas Beecham (to a cellist, attrib.)

Pavarotti is not vain, but conscious of being unique.

> Peter Ustinov

Opera is when a guy gets stabbed in the back and, instead of bleeding, he sings.

> Ed Gardner

The trouble with women in an orchestra is that if they're attractive it will upset my players and if they're not it will upset me.

> Thomas Beecham

Wagner has lovely moments but awful quarters of an hour.

Gioacchino Rossini

～🎵～

Parsifal is the kind of opera that starts at six o'clock. After it has been going three hours, you look at your watch and it says 6.20.

David Randolph

～🎵～

Today if something is not worth saying, people sing it.
Pierre Augustin Caron de Beaumarchais

～🎵～

All music is folk music. I ain't never heard no horse sing a song.

Louis Armstrong

Musical people are so absurdly unreasonable. They always want one to be perfectly dumb at the very moment when one is longing to be absolutely deaf.

Oscar Wilde, *An Ideal Husband*, 1895

I hate music, especially when it's played.

Jimmy Durante

Classic music is th'kind that we keep thinkin'll turn into a tune.

Frank McKinney Hubbard,
Comments of Abe Martin and His Neighbors, 1923

People are wrong when they say that opera is not what it used to be. It is what it used to be. That is what is wrong with it.

Noël Coward

I prefer Offenbach to Bach often.

Thomas Beecham

~•~

There are two golden rules for an orchestra: start together and finish together. The public doesn't give a damn what goes on in between.

Thomas Beecham

~•~

Opera in English is, in the main, just about as sensible as baseball in Italian.

H.L. Mencken

~•~

It is a pity that the composer did not leave directions as to how flat he really did want it sung.

Anon

Mine was the kind of piece in which nobody knew what was going on, including the composer, the conductor and the critics. Consequently I got pretty good notices.

Oscar Levant, *A Smattering of Ignorance*, 1940

Most rock journalism is people who can't write interviewing people who can't talk for people who can't read.

Frank Zappa

"Classic". A book which people praise and don't read.
Mark Twain, *Following the Equator*, 1897

There is a great deal of difference between the eager man who wants to read a book and the tired man who wants a book to read.

G.K. Chesterton

Four happy publishers
Out on a spree
Someone had to pay the bill
And then there were three.

Wendy Cope

I shall lose no time in reading your book.

Benjamin Disraeli

He knew everything about literature except how to
enjoy it.

Joseph Heller, *Catch-22*, 1961

I don't care what is written about me so long as it isn't
true.

Dorothy Parker

Mr J. Ruskin is about to begin a work of great importance and, therefore, begs that in reference to calls and correspondence you will consider him dead for the next two months.

John Ruskin (circular, attrib.)

Once you've put one of his books down, you simply can't pick it up again.

Mark Twain (of Henry James)

Literature is mostly about having sex and not much about having children; life is the other way round.

David Lodge

I've read some of your modern free verse and wonder who set it free.

John Barrymore

Would you convey my compliments to the purist who reads your proofs and tell him or her that I write in a sort of broken-down patois which is something like the way a Swiss waiter talks, and that when I split an infinitive, God damn it, I split it so it will stay split.

Raymond Chandler (to Edward Weeks)

~ ❦ ~

You don't expect me to know what to say about a play when I don't know who the author is, do you?

George Bernard Shaw

~ ❦ ~

When I want to read a novel, I write one.

Benjamin Disraeli

~ ❦ ~

We were put to Dickens as children but it never quite took. That unremitting humanity soon had me cheesed off.

Alan Bennett, *The Old Country*, 1978

The Art of Biography
Is different from Geography
Geography is about maps,
But Biography is about Chaps.

Edmund Clerihew Bentley,
Biography for Beginners, 1905

Critics are to authors what dogs are to lamp-posts.

Jeffrey Robinson

Biography, like big game hunting, is one of the recognized forms of sport, and it is as unfair as only sport can be.

Philip Guedella, *Supers and Supermen*, 1920

Never lend books, for no one ever returns them; the only books I have in my library are books that other folk have lent me.

Anatole France

Yeats is becoming so aristocratic, he's evicting imaginary tenants.

Oliver St John Gogarty

Here is that marriage of style and content we look for in all great writing. A shatteringly vulgar and worthless life captured in shatteringly vulgar and worthless prose.

Stephen Fry, *Paperweight*, 1992

What other culture could have produced someone like Hemingway and not seen the joke?

Gore Vidal

If, with the literate, I am
Impelled to try an epigram,
I never seek to take the credit;
We all assume that Oscar said it.

Dorothy Parker, *A Pig's Eye View of Literature*, 1937

An incinerator is a writer's best friend.

Thornton Wilder

~~❧~~

Writing to a magazine that had published his obituary: I've just read that I am dead. Don't forget to delete me from your list of subscribers.

Rudyard Kipling

~~❧~~

Someone told me that each equation I included in the book would halve the sales.

Stephen Hawking, *A Brief History of Time*, 1988

~~❧~~

I am the most spontaneous speaker in the world because every word, every gesture, and every retort has been carefully rehearsed.

George Bernard Shaw

To H.G. Wells: It is all very well to be able to write books, but can you waggle your ears?

J.M. Barrie

The covers of this book are too far apart.

Ambrose Bierce

I read the book of Job last night. I don't think God comes well out of it.

Virginia Woolf (attrib.)

From a book review: This is not a novel to be tossed aside lightly. It should be thrown with great force.

Dorothy Parker

The profession of book-writing makes horse racing seem like a solid stable business.

John Steinbeck

He directed rehearsals with all the airy deftness of a rheumatic deacon producing Macbeth for a church social.

Noël Coward (of J.R. Crawford, attrib.)

From the moment I picked your book up until the moment I put it down I could not stop laughing. Someday I hope to read it.

Groucho Marx (to Leo Rosten)

It took me fifteen years to discover I had no talent for writing, but I couldn't give it up because by that time I was too famous.

Robert Benchley

An author who speaks about his own books is almost as bad as a mother who talks about her own children.

Benjamin Disraeli

~•~

I have been commissioned to write an autobiography and I would be grateful to any of your readers who could tell me what I was doing between 1960 and 1974.

Jeffrey Bernard

~•~

As to the adjective, when in doubt, strike it out.

Mark Twain, *Pudd'nhead Wilson*, 1894

~•~

I never read the life of any important person without discovering that he knew more and could do more than I could ever hope to know or to do in half a dozen lifetimes.

J.B. Priestley, *Apes and Angels*, 1928

It was like watching someone organize her own immortality. Every phrase and gesture was studied. Now and again, when she said something a little out of the ordinary, she wrote it down herself in a notebook.

Harold Laski (of Virginia Woolf)

~·⦚·~

Dr Donne's verses are like the peace of God; they pass all understanding.

James I

~·⦚·~

One of those big, fat paperbacks, intended to while away a monsoon or two, which, if thrown with a good overarm action, will bring a water buffalo to its knees.

Nancy Banks-Smith (of *The Far Pavilions*)

They told me how Mr Gladstone read Homer for fun, which I thought served him right.

> Winston Churchill, *My Early Life*, 1930

Autobiography is now as common as adultery and hardly less reprehensible.

> John Griff

The art of newspaper paragraphing is to stroke a platitude until it purrs like an epigram.

> Don Marquis

The girl was beheaded, chopped into pieces and placed in a trunk but was not interfered with.

> Newspaper report

A would-be satirist, a hired buffoon,
A monthly scribbler of some low lampoon,
Condemned to drudge, the meanest of the mean,
And furbish falsehoods for a magazine.

Lord Byron

Her journalism, like a diamond, will sparkle more if
it is cut.

Raymond Mortimer (of Susan Sontag)

The good ended happily, and the bad unhappily. That
is what fiction means.

Oscar Wilde, *The Importance of Being Earnest*, 1895

Show me a congenital eavesdropper with the instincts
of a Peeping Tom and I will show you the makings of
a dramatist.

Kenneth Tynan, *Pausing on the Stairs*, 1957

The humour of Dostoievsky is the humour of a bar-loafer who ties a kettle to a dog's tail.

W. Somerset Maugham, *A Writer's Notebook*, 1949

The Compleat Angler is acknowledged to be one of the world's books. Only the trouble is that the world doesn't read its books, it borrows a detective story instead.

Stephen Leacock, *The Boy I Left Behind Me*, 1947

Immature poets imitate; mature poets steal.

T.S. Eliot, *The Sacred Wood*, 1920

Being published by the Oxford University Press is rather like being married to a duchess: the honour is almost greater than the pleasure.

G.M. Young

More than one newspaper has been ruined by the brilliant writer in the editor's chair.

Lord Camrose

~*~

A publisher who writes is like a cow in a milk bar.

Arthur Koestler

~*~

He once telephoned a semicolon from Moscow.

James Bone (on the accuracy of a journalist)

~*~

Freedom of the press in Britain means freedom to print such of the proprietor's prejudices as the advertisers don't object to.

Hannen Swaffer

Nothing induces me to read a novel except when I have to make money by writing about it. I detest them.

Virginia Woolf

If you steal from one author, it's plagiarism; if you steal from many, it's research.

Wilson Mizner

Accuracy to a newspaper is what virtue is to a lady; but a newspaper can always print a retraction.

Adlai Stevenson,
The Wit and Wisdom of Adlai Stevenson, 1965

Let alone re-write, he doesn't even re-read.

Clive James, *The Dreaming Swimmer*, 1992

All bad poetry springs from genuine feeling.

Oscar Wilde

～·{●}·～

For years a secret shame destroyed my peace –
I'd not read Eliot, Auden or MacNeice
But then I had a thought that brought me hope –
Neither had Chaucer, Shakespeare, Milton, Pope.

Justin Richardson, *Take Heart, Illiterates*, 1966

～·{●}·～

I am the kind of writer that people think other people
are reading.

V.S. Naipaul

～·{●}·～

I never read the papers . . . I rely on Sven to tell me if
there's a war broken out. No, I think there's far too
much going on already without reading about it as
well.

Alan Ayckbourn, *Joking Apart*, 1979

No self-respecting fish would be wrapped in a Murdoch newspaper.

Mike Royko

∼⟨●⟩∼

My favourite poem is the one that starts "Thirty days hath September" because it actually tells you something.

Groucho Marx (attrib.)

∼⟨●⟩∼

There are only two styles of portrait painting; the serious and the smirk.

Charles Dickens, *Nicolas Nickleby* 1839

∼⟨●⟩∼

Skill without imagination is craftsmanship and gives us many useful objects such as wickerwork picnic baskets. Imagination without skill gives us modern art.

Tom Stoppard, *Artist Descending a Staircase*, 1972

It is a symbol of Irish art. The cracked lookingglass of a servant.

James Joyce, *Ulysses*, 1922

Most people are vain, so I try to ensure that any author who comes to stay will find at least one of their books in their room.

Duke of Devonshire

There were three things that Chico was always on – a phone, a horse or a broad.

Groucho Marx

Acting is merely the art of keeping a large group of people from coughing.

Ralph Richardson

A verbal contract isn't worth the paper it's written on.

Sam Goldwyn

The play was a great success, but the audience was a total failure.

Oscar Wilde

She took her curtain calls as though she had just been un-nailed from the cross.

Noël Coward (of Edith Evans)

This business is dog eat dog and nobody is gonna eat me.

Sam Goldwyn

Critic's review of the film "Ben-Hur":
Loved Ben, hated Hur.

Anon

Nowadays Mitchum doesn't so much act as point his suit at people.

Russell Davies

It was a cute picture. They used the basic story of Wuthering Heights and worked in surfriders.

Neil Simon, *Last of the Red Hot Lovers*, 1970

We are paid to have dirty minds.

John Trevelyan (when a film censor)

Wet, she was a star – dry she ain't.

Joe Pasternak
(of the swimmer turned actress, Esther Williams)

This might have been good for a picture – except it has too many characters in it.

Wilson Mizner (of the LA phone directory)

Never let the bastard back into my room again – unless I need him.

Sam Goldwyn

Shoot a few scenes out of focus. I want to win the foreign film award.

Billy Wilder (attrib.)

There was laughter in the back of the theatre, leading to the belief that someone was telling jokes back there.

George S. Kaufman

I am suing Lord Beaverbrook for libel and hope for some lovely tax-free money in damages. He has very conveniently told some lies about me.

Evelyn Waugh

I dislike censorship. Like an appendix it is useless when inert and dangerous when active.

Maurice Edelman

I didn't like the play, but then I saw it under adverse conditions – the curtain was up.

Groucho Marx (attrib.)

The trouble with this business is the dearth of bad pictures.

Sam Goldwyn

I wanna be just like you . . . all I need is a lobotomy and some tights.

> Judd Nelson to Emilio Estevez,
> *The Breakfast Club*, 1985

~❀~

A wide screen just makes a bad film twice as bad.

> Sam Goldwyn

~❀~

Lillian Gish may be a charming person, but she is not Ophelia. She comes on stage as if she had been sent for to sew rings on the new curtains.

> Mrs Patrick Campbell

~❀~

I see your schwartz is as big as mine. Now let's see how well you handle it.

> Rick Moranis to Bill Pullman, *Spaceballs*, 1987

Whenever Mrs Kissel breaks wind, we beat the dog.
Max Showlater to Dudley Moore, "*10*", 1979

Are we having fun yet?
Carol Burnett, *Four Seasons*, 1981

That poor man. He's completely unspoiled by failure.
Noël Coward

I'll have what she's having.
Estelle Reiner, *When Harry Met Sally*, 1989

Ya wanna dance or would you rather just suck face?
Henry Fonda to Katharine Hepburn,
On Golden Pond, 1981

Never apologize and never explain – it's a sign of weakness.

John Wayne, *She Wore a Yellow Ribbon*, 1949

~⚓~

Try the cock, Albert. It's a delicacy, and you know where it's been.

Helen Mirren,
The Cook, The Thief, His Wife and Her Lover, 1990

~⚓~

God always has another custard pie up His sleeve.

Lynn Redgrave, *Georgy Girl*, 1966

~⚓~

I have to go now. I'm having an old friend for dinner.

Anthony Hopkins, *Silence of the Lambs*, 1990

~⚓~

When asked what he looked for in a film script: Days off.

Spencer Tracy

You can pick out actors by the glazed look that comes into their eyes when the conversation wanders away from themselves.

Michael Wilding

On being asked how old he was: I am just turning forty and taking my time about it.

Harold Lloyd

Once you've been really bad in a movie, there's a certain kind of fearlessness you develop.

Jack Nicholson

When I grow up, I still want to be a director.

Steven Spielberg

I grew up with six brothers. That's how I learned to dance – waiting for the bathroom.

Bob Hope

~•~

All my shows are great. Some of them are bad. But they are all great.

Lord Grade

~•~

Behind the phoney tinsel of Hollywood lies the real tinsel.

Oscar Levant

~•~

Television? The word is half Greek, half Latin. No good can come of it.

C.P. Scott

It is astonishing how articulate one can become when alone and raving at a radio. Arguments and counter arguments, rhetoric and bombast flow from one's lips like scurf from the hair of a bank manager.

Stephen Fry, *Paperweight*, 1992

To an actor: My dear boy, forget about the motivation. Just say the lines and don't trip over the furniture.

Noël Coward

Gary Cooper and Greta Garbo may be the same person. Have you ever seen them together?

Ernst Lubitsch

My brain? It's my second favorite organ.
Woody Allen and Marshall Brickman, *Sleeper*, 1973

I suppose you know you have a wonderful body. I'd like to do it in clay.

Lola Albright to Kirk Douglas, *Champion*, 1949

~ 🌰 ~

It's amazing how many people see you on TV. I did my first television show a month ago, and the next day five million television sets were sold. The people who couldn't sell theirs threw them away.

Bob Hope

~ 🌰 ~

Television: A medium. So called because it is neither rare nor well done.

Ernie Kovacs

~ 🌰 ~

Television is simultaneously blamed, often by the same people, for worsening the world and for being powerless to change it.

Clive James, *Glued to the Box*, 1981

I told you 158 times I cannot stand little notes on my pillow. "We are out of cornflakes. F.U." It took me three hours to figure out F.U. was Felix Ungar. It's not your fault Felix: it's a rotten combination that's all.

Walter Matthau to Jack Lemmon,
The Odd Couple, 1968

I hate the beach. I hate the sun. I'm pale and I'm redheaded. I don't tan – I stroke!

Woody Allen, *Play it Again Sam*, 1972

The only question I ever ask any woman is: What time is your husband coming home?

Paul Newman to Patricia Neal, *Hud*, 1963

Chapter 2

WOMEN

Once a woman has given you her heart, you can never get rid of the rest of her body.
John Vanbrugh, *The Relapse*, 1696

A woman without a man is like a fish without a bicycle.
Gloria Steinem (attrib.)

Too much has been said and recorded about women not to give them their own category; whether women are being funny about themselves or being made fun of, it provides a scintillating ping-pong of insults and counter-insults, invective and braggadocio.

Women's clothes: never wear anything that panics the cat.

P.J. O'Rourke, *Modern Manners*, 1984

Show me a woman who doesn't feel guilt and I'll show you a man.

Erica Jong

Claudia's the sort of girl who goes through life holding onto the sides.

Alice Thomas Ellis, *The Other Side of the Fire*, 1983

Nature has given women so much power that the law has very wisely given them little.

Samuel Johnson

I only know that people call me a feminist whenever I express sentiments that differentiate me from a doormat or a prostitute.

Rebecca West, *The Young Rebecca*, 1982

~§~

Give a woman an inch and she thinks she's a ruler.

Anon

~§~

Most women loathe limericks, for the same reason that calves hate cookbooks.

Gershon Legman

~§~

I don't want to talk grammar, I want to talk like a lady.

George Bernard Shaw, *Pygmalion*, 1916

Pat: Whenever I'm down in the dumps, I get myself another hat.
Sue: I wondered where you found them.

Anon

Being an old maid is like death by drowning, a really delightful sensation after you cease to struggle.

Edna Ferber

As long as a woman can look ten years younger than her own daughter, she is perfectly satisfied.

Oscar Wilde, *The Picture of Dorian Gray*, 1891

She looked like a huge ball of fur on two well-developed legs. Shortest dress I ever saw and a Frenchman said it begins so low and ends so soon.

Nancy Mitford (of Princess Margaret)

It is possible that blondes also prefer gentlemen.

Mamie Van Doren

Whatever women do, they must do twice as well as men to be thought half as good. Luckily, this is not difficult.

Charlotte Whitton

I'm the girl who lost her reputation and never missed it.

Mae West

If you are flattering a woman, it pays to be a little more subtle. You don't have to bother with men, they believe any compliment automatically.

Alan Ayckbourn, *Round and Round the Garden*, 1975

How much fame, money and power does a woman have to achieve on her own before you can punch her in the face?

P.J. O'Rourke, *Modern Manners*, 1984

The hardest task in a girl's life is to prove to a man that his intentions are serious.

Helen Rowland

Our aunts and grandmothers always tell us men are a sort of animal, that if ever they are constant 'tis only where they are ill used.

Lady Wortley Montagu

A woman who strives to be like a man lacks ambition.

Anon

She plucked from my lapel the invisible strand of lint
(the universal act of women to proclaim ownership).

O. Henry

~ 🔔 ~

When women kiss it always reminds one of prize-
fighters shaking hands.

H.L. Mencken, *Chrestomathy*, 1949

~ 🔔 ~

Someone you like is wearing an ugly hat, and she asks
you to give her your honest opinion of it:
"What a lovely chapeau! But if I may make one teensy
suggestion? If it blows off, don't chase it."

Miss Piggy, *Miss Piggy's Guide to Life*, 1981

~ 🔔 ~

If a woman hasn't met the right man by the time she's
twenty-four, she may be lucky.

Deborah Kerr

In her early days she had that beatific expression characteristic of Victorian prettiness – like a sheep painted by Raphael.

James Agate (of Lillie Langtry)

This was an actress who, for twenty years, had the world at her feet. She kicked it away, and the ball rolled out of her reach.

James Agate (of Mrs Patrick Campbell)

One of the reasons I don't see eye to eye with Women's Lib is that women have it all on a plate if only they knew it. They don't have to be pretty either.

Charlotte Rampling

Plain women he regarded as he did the other severe facts of life, to be faced with philosophy and investigated by science.

George Eliot, *Middlemarch*, 1872

No woman is worth more than a fiver unless you're in love with her. Then she's worth all she costs you.

W. Somerset Maugham, *A Writer's Notebook*, 1949

She does not understand the concept of Roman numerals. She thought we just fought World War Eleven.

Joan Rivers

A woman is no sooner ours than we are no longer hers.

Montaigne

A woman occasionally is quite a serviceable substitute for masturbation. It takes an abundance of imagination, to be sure.

Karl Kraus

I used to think it a pity that her mother rather than she had not thought of birth control.

Muriel Spark (of Marie Stopes)

Rich widows: The only secondhand goods that sell at first-class prices.

Benjamin Franklin

She is a peacock in everything but beauty.

Oscar Wilde

'Tis strange what a man may do, and a woman yet think him an angel.

William Makepeace Thackery,
The History of Henry Esmond, 1852

I'm tired of all this nonsense about beauty being only skin-deep. That's deep enough. What do you want – an adorable pancreas?

Jean Kerr, *The Snake has all the Lines*, 1958

I used to be Snow White, but I drifted.

Mae West (attrib.)

The fickleness of the women I love is only equalled by the infernal constancy of the women who love me.

George Bernard Shaw

The body of a young woman is God's greatest achievement . . . Of course, He could have built it to last longer but you can't have everything.

Neil Simon, *Gingerbread Lady*, 1970

All women become like their mothers. That is their tragedy. No man does. That's his.

Oscar Wilde, *The Importance of Being Earnest*, 1895

High heels were invented by a woman who had been kissed on the forehead.

Christopher Morley

The rich man and his daughter are soon parted.

Frank McKinney Hubbard

My executive often arrives at the apartment exhausted and emotionally detached after a hard day of corporate manipulation and chicanery. He depends on me to raise his lowered interest rate and stimulate his private sector.

Off The Wall Street Journal, 1982

Women's styles may change but their designs remain
the same.

Oscar Wilde

~ ¿&. ~

I've only slept with the men I've been married to. How
many women can make that claim?

Elizabeth Taylor

~ ¿&. ~

Her interest in natural history was confined to
observation of the crows' feet gathering around her
eyes.

Nicholas Bentley

~ ¿&. ~

When women go wrong, men go right after them.
Mae West, *She Done Him Wrong*, 1933

She looked as if she had been poured into her clothes
and had forgotten to say when.

P.G. Wodehouse

~·&·~

One can find women who have never had one love
affair, but it is rare indeed to find any who have had
only one.

François de La Rouchefoucauld

~·&·~

Her cooking suggested she had attended the Cordon
Noir.

Leo Rosten

~·&·~

She wore a low but futile décolletage.

Dorothy Parker

Sure, deck your lower limbs in pants;
Yours are the limbs, my sweeting.
You look divine as you advance –
Have you seen yourself retreating?

Ogden Nash, *What's the Use*, 1940

A woman can keep one secret – the secret of her age.

Voltaire

She laughs at everything you say. Why? Because she has fine teeth.

Benjamin Franklin

After forty a woman has to choose between losing her figure or her face. My advice is to keep your face, and stay sitting down.

Barbara Cartland

Her capacity for family affection is extraordinary. When her third husband died, her hair turned quite gold from grief.

    Oscar Wilde, *The Picture of Dorian Gray*, 1891

A vacuum with nipples.

    Otto Preminger (of Marilyn Monroe)

An archaeologist is the best husband a woman can have: the older she gets, the more interested he is in her.

    Agatha Christie

Burt Reynolds once asked me out. I was in his room.

    Phyllis Diller

When he is late for dinner and I know he must be either having an affair or lying dead in the street, I always hope he's dead.

Judith Viorst

There are a number of mechanical devices which increase sexual arousal, particularly in women. Chief among these is the Mercedes-Benz 380SL convertible.

P.J. O'Rourke, *Modern Manners*, 1984

Woman begins by resisting a man's advances and ends by blocking his retreat.

Oscar Wilde

Chapter 3

SEX, LOVE, MARRIAGE & CHILDREN

The first half of our life is ruined by our
parents and the second half by our children.
Clarence Darrow

*Love makes the world go round – love and all its inevitable
by-products (sex, marriage, children . . .) and provides an
infinite stock of droll, if rather cynical, quotations.*

Some people ask the secret of our long marriage. We take time to go to a restaurant two times a week. A little candlelight, dinner, soft music and dancing. She goes Tuesdays, I go Fridays.

Henny Youngman

The good thing about masturbation is that you don't have to dress up for it.

Truman Capote

To fall in love you have to be in the state of mind for it to take, like a disease.

Nancy Mitford

She was just a passing fiancée.

Alfred McFote

Parents: people who use the rhythm method of birth control.

May Flink

Marriage has driven more than one man to sex.

Peter de Vries

Religion has done love a great service by making it a sin.

Anatole France

Four be the things I'd been better without:
Love, curiosity, freckles, and doubt.

Dorothy Parker, *Inventory*, 1937

If you are truly serious about preparing your child for the future, don't teach him to subtract, teach him to deduct.

Fran Lebowitz, *Social Studies*, 1981

～💧～

Ah Mozart! He was happily married – but his wife wasn't.

Victor Borge

～💧～

Where does the family start? It starts with a young man falling in love with a girl – no superior alternative has yet been found.

Winston Churchill (attrib.)

～💧～

Husbands: a small band of men, armed only with wallets, besieged by a horde of wives and children.

National Lampoon, 1979

Adultery is the application of democracy to love.
H.L. Mencken, *Senteniae*, 1920

Sex is the thing that takes up the least amount of time and causes the most amount of trouble.
John Barrymore

The three most important events of human life are equally devoid of reason: birth, marriage and death.
Austin O'Malley

A man can be happy with any woman as long as he does not love her.
Oscar Wilde, *The Picture of Dorian Gray*, 1891

Paying alimony is like feeding hay to a dead horse.
Groucho Marx

He's dreadfully married. He's the most married man I ever saw in my life.

Artemus Ward

~;&~

Going to bed with a woman never hurt a ballplayer. It's staying up all night looking for them that does you in.

Casey Stengel

~;&~

Do you know what it means to come home at night to a woman who'll give you a little love, a little affection, a little tenderness? It means you're in the wrong house, that's what it means.

George Burns

~;&~

Behind every successful man stands a surprised mother-in-law.

Hubert Humphrey

If it weren't for pickpockets I'd have no sex-life at all.

Rodney Dangerfield

Love: a temporary insanity curable by marriage.

Ambrose Bierce

Getting divorced just because you don't love a man is almost as silly as getting married just because you do.

Zsa Zsa Gabor

If we take matrimony at its lowest, we regard it as a sort of friendship recognized by the police.

Robert Louis Stevenson

If parents would only realize how they bore their children.

George Bernard Shaw,
Everybody's Political What's What?, 1944

In Spain, lust is in the air. There is nothing clandestine about the Spanish appreciation of sex, nothing inhibited or restrained. That is why there are very few sexual crimes in Spain.

Fernand Diaz-Plaja

If love is the answer, could you rephrase the question?

Lily Tomlin

I said to the wife, "Guess what I heard in the pub? They reckon the milkman has made love to every woman in our road except one." And she said, "I'll bet it's that stuck-up Phyllis at number 23."

Max Kauffmann

Many a man has fallen in love with a girl in a light so dim he would not have chosen a suit by it.

Maurice Chevalier

Love is what happens to a man and woman who don't know each other.

W. Somerset Maugham

When I can no longer bear to think of the victims of broken homes, I begin to think of the victims of intact ones.

Peter de Vries

Happiness is having a large, loving, caring, close-knit family in another city.

George Burns

Bigamy is having one wife too many. Monogamy is the same.

Oscar Wilde

Men have a much better time of it than women; for one thing they marry later; for another thing they die earlier.

H.L. Mencken

~ 🐝 ~

Insanity is hereditary. You get it from your children.

Sam Levenson

~ 🐝 ~

When I was fourteen, my father was so ignorant I could hardly stand to have him around. When I got to be twenty-one, I was astonished at how much he had learned in seven years.

Mark Twain

~ 🐝 ~

The big difference between sex for money and sex for free is that sex for money usually costs less.

Brendan Francis

Papa loved Mamma
Mamma loved men
Mamma's in the graveyard
Papa's in the pen.

Carl Sandburg

As to marriage or celibacy, let a man take which course he will. He will be sure to repent.

Socrates

Well, they use their tongues, foreign implements, eventually reach orgasm. And they quarrel about the condition of the room, and go out to a French movie. It's what makes them happy.

Bob Ellis to Norman Kaye, *Man of Flowers*, 1984

It's hard for me to get used to these changing times. I can remember when the air was clean and sex was dirty.

George Burns

Young men want to be faithful, and are not; old men want to be faithless, and cannot.

Oscar Wilde, *The Picture of Dorian Gray*, 1891

❧

I'm afraid I was very much the traditionalist. I went down on one knee and dictated a proposal which my secretary faxed over straight away.

Stephen Fry and Hugh Laurie

❧

I haven't spoken to my wife in years – I didn't want to interrupt her.

Rodney Dangerfield

❧

Marriage is always popular because it combines the maximum of temptation with the maximum of opportunity.

George Bernard Shaw

If this is foreplay, I'm a dead man!

Steve Guttenberg, *Cocoon*, 1985

Love is only the dirty trick played on us to achieve continuation of the species.

W. Somerset Maugham, *A Writer's Notebook*, 1949

My computer dating bureau came up with a perfect gentleman. Still, I've got another three goes.

Sally Poplin

There's nothing wrong with pregnancy. Half the people wouldn't be here today if it wasn't for women being pregnant.

Sarah Kennedy

Never lend your car to anyone to whom you have given birth.

Erma Bombeck

~ ❦ ~

The four stages of man are infancy, childhood, adolescence and obsolescence.

Art Linkletter,
A Child's Garden of Misinformation, 1965

~ ❦ ~

If you have a child who is seven feet tall, you don't cut off his head or his legs. You buy him a bigger bed and hope he plays basketball.

Robert Altman

~ ❦ ~

Somewhere on this globe, every ten seconds, there is a woman giving birth to a child. She must be found and stopped.

Sam Levenson

What is commonly called love, namely the desire of satisfying a voracious appetite with a certain quantity of delicate white human flesh.

Henry Fielding, *Tom Jones*, 1749

Marriage is the alliance of two people, one of whom never remembers birthdays and the other never forgets them.

Ogden Nash

I like children. If they're properly cooked.

W.C. Fields

It is now quite lawful for a Catholic woman to avoid pregnancy by a resort to mathematics, though she is still forbidden to resort to physics or chemistry.

H.L. Mencken

What is a promiscuous person? It's usually someone who is getting more sex than you are.

Victor Lownes, *Playboy*

~{&.~

It is better to copulate than never.

Robert Heinlein

~{&.~

There is no reciprocity. Men love women, women love children, children love hamsters.

Alice Thomas Ellis

~{&.~

Parents should conduct their arguments in quiet, respectful tones, but in a foreign language. You'd be surprised what an inducement that is to the education of children.

Judith Martin

Love is much nicer to be in than an automobile accident, a tight girdle, a higher tax bracket or a holding pattern over Philadelphia.

Judith Viorst, *Redbook*, 1975

Every luxury was lavished on you – atheism, breastfeeding, circumcision.

Joe Orton, *Loot*, 1967

My parents were very pleased that I was in the army. The fact that I hated it somehow pleased them even more.

Barry Humphries, *More Please*, 1992

Never tell a loved one about an infidelity . . . Although one dislikes being deceived, one likes even less to be undeceived.

Nino de Lanclos

Ask your child what he wants for dinner only if he's buying.

Fran Lebowitz, *Social Studies*, 1981

~ ♠ ~

Father doesn't hear what Mother says, and Mother hears what Father does not say.

Anon

~ ♠ ~

I doubt that art needed Ruskin any more than a moving train needs one of its passengers to shove it.

Tom Stoppard

~ ♠ ~

Before permissiveness came in, everyone everywhere was at it like randy goats. But the moment the young started to insist on talking about it all the time, you couldn't get laid if you were a table at the Savoy.

Stephen Fry, *Hippopotamus*, 1994

I'm all for bringing back the birch, but only between consenting adults.

Gore Vidal

Marrying a man is like buying something you've been admiring for a long time in a shop window. You may love it when you get it home, but it doesn't always go with everything else.

Jean Kerr

I wasn't kissing her, I was just whispering in her mouth.

Chico Marx

I've been around so long, I knew Doris Day before she was a virgin.

Groucho Marx

No, no; for my virginity,
When I lose that, says Rose, I'll die:
Behind the elms last night, cried Dick,
Rose, were you not extremely sick?

Matthew Prior, *A True Maid*, 1718

Children and zip fasteners do not respond to force
... Except occasionally.

Katharine Whitehorn, *Observations*, 1970

A child of one can be taught not to do certain things
such as touch a hot stove, turn on the gas, pull lamps
off the tables by their cords, or wake Mommy before
noon.

Joan Rivers

Love is not looking in each other's eyes, but looking
together in the same direction.

Antoine de Saint-Exupéry

Parents should be given only a modest and sensible allowance. And they should be encouraged to save up for things. This builds character. It also helps pay for the funeral.

P.J. O'Rourke, *Modern Manners*, 1984

Nobody in their right mind would call me a nymphomaniac. I only sleep with good-looking men.

Fiona Pitt-Kethley

She kissed her way into society. I don't like her. But don't misunderstand me: my dislike is purely platonic.

Herbert Beerbohm Tree

It is true from early habit, one must make love mechanically as one swims. I was once very fond of both, but now as I never swim unless I tumble into the water, I don't make love till almost obliged.

Lord Byron

Masturbation: the primary sexual activity of mankind. In the nineteenth century, it was a disease; in the twentieth, it's a cure.

Thomas Szasz, *The Second Sin*, 1973

Chapter 4

SOCIAL COMMENT

'Tis often thus with simple folk - an accepted wit has but to say "Pass the mustard", and they roar their ribs out!
    W.S. Gilbert, *The Yeoman of the Guard*, 1888

A miscellany of satirical observations on the vagaries of society and its machinations.

Nothing is more irritating than not being invited to a party you wouldn't be seen dead at.

Bill Vaughan

~❦~

Luck is a matter of preparation meeting opportunity.

Oprah Winfrey

~❦~

We must believe in luck. For how else can we explain the success of those we don't like.

Jean Cocteau

~❦~

All you need in this life is ignorance and confidence, and then success is sure.

Mark Twain

It drives me to a frothing frenzy when politicians return from inner cities saying: "What the people of this town need is Hope", as if we could all respond with a glad cry of "No sooner said than done old sport", as we gather up a handful of Hope from the sideboard, stuff it into a Jiffy-bag and send it off to Liverpool 8 by the First Class Post. What these bleeding hearts mean is Money, but they're too greasy to say so.

Stephen Fry, *Hippopotamus*, 1994

Wickedness is a myth invented by good people to account for the curious attractiveness of others.

Oscar Wilde

It is a secret in the Oxford sense. You may tell it to only one person at a time.

Lord Franks

There are two times in a man's life when he should not speculate: when he can't afford it, and when he can.

Mark Twain

~ ❧ ~

All that I desire to point out is the general principle that Life imitates Art far more than Art imitates Life.

Oscar Wilde

~ ❧ ~

He who laughs, lasts.

Mary Pettibone Poole

~ ❧ ~

I do not see any reason why the devil should have all the good tunes.

Rowland Hill

I must decline your invitation owing to a subsequent invitation.

Oscar Wilde

The scientific theory I like best is that the rings of Saturn are composed entirely of lost airline baggage.

Mark Russell

If a scientist were to cut his ear off, no one would take it as evidence of a heightened sensibility.

Peter Medawar

Duty is what one expects from others, it is not what one does oneself.

Oscar Wilde, *A Woman of No Importance*, 1893

I was gratified to be able to answer promptly. I said I don't know.

Mark Twain

～⋅⋅⋅～

Living with a saint is more gruelling than being one.

Robert Neville

～⋅⋅⋅～

Never assume that habitual silence means ability in reserve.

Geoffrey Madan, *Twelve Reflections*, 1934

～⋅⋅⋅～

A conference is a gathering of important people who singly can do nothing, but together can decide that nothing can be done.

Fred Allen

Saturday afternoon, although occurring at regular and well-forseen intervals, always takes this railway by surprise.

W.S. Gilbert

There is something fascinating about silence. One gets such wholesale returns of conjecture out of such a trifling investment of fact.

Mark Twain

The worse part of having success is to try finding someone who is happy for you.

Bette Midler (attrib.)

People who work sitting down get paid more than people who work standing up.

Ogden Nash

We owe a lot to Thomas Edison – if it wasn't for him, we'd be watching television by candlelight.

Milton Berle

This is a free country, madam. We have a right to share your privacy in a public place.

Peter Ustinov, *Romanoff and Juliet*, 1956

Manners are especially the need of the plain. The pretty can get away with anything.

Evelyn Waugh

When a person tells you, "I'll think it over and let you know" – you know.

Olin Miller

If all economists were laid end to end, they would not reach a conclusion.

George Bernard Shaw

~ ❦ ~

The right to be heard does not include the right to be taken seriously.

Hubert Humphrey

~ ❦ ~

That indefatigable and unsavoury engine of pollution, the dog.

John Sparrow

~ ❦ ~

I want nothing to do with any religion concerned with keeping the masses satisfied to live in hunger, filth and ignorance.

Jawaharlal Nehru

Racism is man's gravest threat to man — the maximum of hatred for the minimum of reason.

Abraham Joshua Heschel

The trouble with the world is that the stupid are cocksure and the intelligent full of doubt.

Bertrand Russell

It is absurd to divide people into good and bad. People are either charming or tedious.

Oscar Wilde

All religions are founded on the fear of the many and the cleverness of the few.

Stendhal

If men are so wicked with religion, what would they be without it?

Benjamin Franklin

～⧼⧽～

Nothing needs so reforming as other people's habits.

Mark Twain

～⧼⧽～

Reality is for people who can't face drugs.

Laurence Peter

～⧼⧽～

Nothing is more annoying than to be obscurely hanged.

Voltaire

～⧼⧽～

It is difficult to see why lace should be so expensive; it is mostly holes.

Mary Wilson Little

It is perfectly monstrous the way people go about nowadays saying things against one, behind one's back, that are absolutely and entirely true.

Oscar Wilde

~•~

The liar's punishment is not in the least that he is not believed but that he cannot believe anyone else.

George Bernard Shaw

~•~

Any fool can tell the truth, but it requires a man of some sense to know how to lie well.

Samuel Butler

~•~

There are people so addicted to exaggeration that they can't tell the truth without lying.

Josh Billings

A lie can be halfway round the world before the truth has got its boots on.

James Callaghan

How come there's only one Monopolies Commission?

Nigel Rees, *Graffiti 4*, 1982

The way to ensure summer in England is to have it framed and glazed in a comfortable room.

Horace Walpole

Kitchener is a great poster.

Margot Asquith, *More Memories*, 1933

A door is what a dog is perpetually on the wrong side of.

Ogden Nash,
A Dog's Best Friend is his Illiteracy, 1953

~·§·~

One should never make one's entrance with a scandal. One should reserve that to give an interest to one's old age.

Oscar Wilde, *The Picture of Dorian Gray*, 1891

~·§·~

I don't at all like knowing what people say of me behind my back. It makes one far too conceited.

Oscar Wilde, *An Ideal Husband*, 1895

~·§·~

The physician can bury his mistakes, but the architect can only advise his client to plant vines.

Frank Lloyd Wright

We're living in an age where you have to call a chick and ask her if she'll wear a dress tonight. And she says: "You're weird."

Tim Rose

If not actually disgruntled, he was far from being gruntled.

P.G. Wodehouse

Gold was not altogether certain what, anatomically, a gorge was, but he knew that his was rising.

Joseph Heller, *Good as Gold*, 1979

A chrysanthemum by any other name would be easier to spell.

William J. Johnston

The dusk was performing its customary intransitive operation of "gathering".

Flann O'Brien, *The Best of Myles*, 1968

Space isn't remote at all. It's only an hour's drive away if your car could go straight upwards.

Sir Fred Hoyle

Some cause happiness wherever they go; others whenever they go.

Oscar Wilde

The gambling known as business looks with austere disfavour upon the business known as gambling.

Ambrose Bierce

Committees are a group of the unfit appointed by the unwilling to do the unnecessary.

Carl C. Byers

~·⦂·~

I remember your name perfectly, but I just can't think of your face.

Reverend William Spooner

~·⦂·~

You have tasted your worm, you have hissed my mystery lectures, and you must leave by the first town drain.

Reverend William Spooner

~·⦂·~

You're the sort of person Dr Spooner would have called a shining wit!

Anon

I know two things about the horse
And one of them is rather coarse.

Naomi Royde-Smith

Do you recollect the poodle – exactly like a typhoid germ magnified.

George Lyttelton

Let's find out what everyone is doing,
And then stop everyone from doing it.

A.P. Herbert

A jury consists of twelve persons chosen to decide who has the better lawyer.

Robert Frost

Everyone likes flattery and when you come to Royalty you should lay it on with a trowel.

Benjamin Disraeli (attrib.)

Unseen, in the background, Fate was quietly slipping the lead into the boxing glove.

P.G. Wodehouse, *Very Good Jeeves*, 1930

We should take care not to make the intellect our god; it has, of course, powerful muscles, but no personality.

Albert Einstein

All our final decisions are made in a state of mind that is not going to last.

Marcel Proust

It is a good rule in life never to apologize. The right sort of people do not want apologies, and the wrong sort take a mean advantage of them.

P.G. Wodehouse, *The Man Upstairs*, 1914

I hate to advocate drugs, alcohol, violence, or insanity to anyone, but they've always worked for me.

Hunter S. Thompson

Art is I; science is we.

Claude Bernard

What they call "heart" lies much lower than the fourth waistcoat button.

George Lichtenberg

A successful lawsuit is one worn by a policeman.

Robert Frost

Fashion is what one wears oneself. What is unfashionable is what other people wear.

Oscar Wilde, *An Ideal Husband*, 1895

Critics are like eunuchs in a harem: they know how it's done, they've seen it done every day, but they're unable to do it themselves.

Brendan Behan (attrib.)

We must respect the other fellow's religion, but only in the sense and to the extent that we respect his theory that his wife is beautiful and his children smart.

H.L. Mencken

Honest criticism is hard to take, particularly from a relative, a friend, an acquaintance or a stranger.

Franklin P. Jones

～‌‌～

Never buy anything simply because it is expensive.

Oscar Wilde

～‌‌～

The price of freedom of religion, or of speech, or of the press, is that we must put up with a good deal of rubbish.

Robert Jackson

～‌‌～

In matters of grave importance, style, not sincerity, is the vital thing.

Oscar Wilde, *The Importance of Being Earnest*, 1895

You will always find some Eskimo ready to instruct the Congolese on how to cope with heatwaves.

Stanislaw J. Lec

The most beautiful things in the world are the most useless – peacocks and lilies, for instance.

John Ruskin

It is better to keep your mouth shut and to appear stupid than to open it and remove all doubt.

Mark Twain

A celebrity is a person who works hard all his life to become well known, then wears dark glasses to avoid being recognized.

Fred Allen

Eccentricity, to be socially acceptable, had still to have at least four or five generations of inbreeding behind it.

Osbert Lancaster, *All Done From Memory*, 1953

Lots of folks confuse bad management with destiny.

Frank McKinney Hubbard

Only the shallow know themselves.

Oscar Wilde

I'd rather be black than gay because when you're black you don't have to tell your mother.

Charles Pierce

The word "good" has many meanings. For example, if a man were to shoot his grandmother at a range of five hundred yards, I should call him a good shot, but not necessarily a good man.

G.K. Chesterton

The fellow who laughs last may laugh best, but he gets the reputation of being very slow-witted.

Leo Rosten

When you are in trouble, people who call to sympathize are really looking for the particulars.

Edgar Watson Howe, *Country Town Sayings*, 1911

Psychiatry enables us to correct our faults by confessing our parent's shortcomings.

Laurence Peter

Jogging is for people who aren't intelligent enough to watch television.

Victoria Wood

It's my rule never to lose me temper till it would be detrimental to keep it.

Sean O'Casey, *The Plough and the Stars*, 1926

Income tax has made more liars out of the American people than golf.

Will Rogers

The penalty of success is to be bored by the people who used to snub you.

Nancy Astor

Good taste is better than bad taste, but bad taste is better than no taste.

Arnold Bennett

Your friend is the man who knows all about you, and still likes you.

Elbert Hubbard, *The Notebook*, 1927

Let's forget about the six feet and talk about the seven inches.

Mae West

The trouble with being in the rat-race is that even if you win, you're still a rat.

Lily Tomlin

The old middle-class prerogative of being permanently in a most filthy temper.

John Mortimer, *Clinging to the Wreckage*, 1982

A man who moralizes is usually a hypocrite, and a woman who moralizes is invariably plain.

Oscar Wilde, *Lady Windermere's Fan*, 1892

He has all the characteristics of a dog – except loyalty.

Sam Houston

When everyone is somebodee,
Then no one's anybody.

W.S. Gilbert, *The Gondoliers*, 1889

The man who is denied the opportunity of taking decisions of importance begins to regard as important the decisions he is allowed to take.

    C. Northcote Parkinson, *Parkinson's Law*, 1958

The opposite of talking isn't listening. The opposite of talking is waiting.

    Fran Lebowitz, *Social Studies*, 1981

Impotence and sodomy are socially o.k. but birth control is flagrantly middle-class.

    Evelyn Waugh

The good are so harsh to the clever, the clever so rude to the good.

    Miss Wordsworth

A camel is a horse designed by a committee.

Alec Issigonis

There are two things to aim at in this life; first to get what you want; and, after that, to enjoy it. Only the wisest of mankind achieve the second.

Logan Pearsall Smith

All beginnings are delightful; the threshold is the place to pause.

Goethe

Don't talk about naval tradition. It's nothing but rum, sodomy, and the lash.

Winston Churchill

Give a civil servant a good cause and he'll wreck it with clichés, bad punctuation, double negatives and convoluted apology.

Alan Clark

I'd like to borrow his body for just 48 hours. There are three guys I'd like to beat up and four women I'd like to make love to.

Jim Murray (of Muhammad Ali)

If you obey all the rules, you miss all the fun.

Katharine Hepburn

When a man wants to murder a tiger he calls it sport; when a tiger wants to murder him, he calls it ferocity.

George Bernard Shaw, *Man and Superman*, 1903

Moral indignation is jealousy with a halo.

H.G. Wells

~·&·~

To keep an organization young and fit, don't hire anyone until everybody's so overworked they'll be glad to see the newcomer no matter where he sits.

Robert Townsend

~·&·~

It's a recession when your neighbor loses his job; it's a depression when you lose yours.

Harry S. Truman

~·&·~

You must come again when you have less time.

Walter Sickert

An aristocracy in a republic is like a chicken whose head has been cut off: it may run about in a lively way, but in fact it is dead.

Nancy Mitford

Good manners is the art of making those people easy with whom we converse. Whoever makes the fewest people uneasy is the best bred in the company.

Jonathan Swift

Never take a reference from a clergyman. They always want to give someone a second chance.

Lady Selborne

Life is a mirror: if you frown at it, it frowns back; if you smile, it returns the greeting.

William Makepeace Thackeray

Anybody seen in a bus over the age of thirty has been a failure in life.

Loelia, Duchess of Westminster

Be civil to all; sociable to many; familiar with few.

Benjamin Disraeli

He that has a secret to hide should not only hide it but hide that he has it to hide.

Thomas Carlyle

It is very strange, and very melancholy, that the paucity of human pleasures should persuade us ever to call hunting one of them.

Samuel Johnson

Friends are God's apology for relations.

Hugh Kingsmill

~❧~

The one important thing I have learned over the years is the difference between taking one's work seriously and taking one's self seriously. The first is imperative and the second is disastrous.

Margot Fonteyn

~❧~

The world is a comedy to those who think, a tragedy to those who feel.

Horace Walpole

~❧~

Never go out to meet trouble. If you will just sit still, nine cases out of ten someone will intercept it before it reaches you.

Calvin Coolidge

How many cares one loses when one decides not to be something, but to be someone.

Coco Chanel

All decent people live beyond their incomes nowadays, and those who aren't respectable live beyond other people's.

Saki, *Chronicles of Clovis*, 1911

Like all weak men he laid an exaggerated stress on not changing one's mind.

W. Somerset Maugham, *Of Human Bondage*, 1915

Laugh and the world laughs with you. Snore and you sleep alone.

Anthony Burgess

If you can keep your head while those about you are losing theirs, perhaps you do not understand the situation.

Nelson Boswell

Work is the curse of the drinking classes.

Oscar Wilde

A house unkept cannot be so distressing as a life unlived.

Rose Macaulay

Remember that as a teenager you are at the last stage in your life when you will be happy to hear that the phone is for you.

Fran Lebowitz, *Social Studies*, 1981

Like all very selfish people she slipped easily into the role of martyr.

> Christopher Sykes (of Lady William Russell)

Age is deformed, youth unkind,
We scorn their bodies, they our mind.

> Thomas Bastard, *Chrestoleros*

Listen. Say less rather than more. If you want to be smart, play stupid!

> Helena Rubenstein

Never trust a man who combs his hair straight from his left armpit.

> Alice Roosevelt Longworth

The world is divided into people who do things and people who get the credit. Try, if you can, to belong to the first class. There's far less competition.

Dwight Morrow

Please don't talk while I am interrupting.

Todd Rockefeller

Hindsight is always twenty-twenty.

Billy Wilder

Please don't talk while I am interrupting.

One has to resign oneself to being a nuisance if one wants to get anything done.

Freya Stark

I am afraid that he has one of those terribly weak natures that are not susceptible to influence.

Oscar Wilde, *An Ideal Husband*, 1895

Happiness is nothing more than good health and a bad memory.

Albert Schweitzer

~⟨●⟩~

What is the difference between a taxidermist and a tax collector? The taxidermist takes only your skin.

Mark Twain

~⟨●⟩~

The less one has to do the less time one finds to do it.

Anon

~⟨●⟩~

Work expands so as to fill the time available for its completion.

C. Northcote Parkinson, *Parkinson's Law*, 1958

We have in England a curious belief in first-rate people, meaning all the people we do not know; and this consoles us for the undeniable second-rateness of the people we do know.

George Bernard Shaw, *The Irrational Knot*, 1905

Ice formed on the butler's upper slopes.

P.G. Wodehouse, *Pigs Have Wings*, 1952

If you have nothing good to say about anyone, come and sit by me.

Alice Roosevelt Longworth

The trouble with high-tech is that you always end up using scissors.

David Hockney

A little inaccuracy sometimes saves tons of explanation.

Saki, The Square Egg, 1924

~ི༠ི~

It's true hard work never killed anybody, but I figure why take the chance?

Ronald Reagan

~ི༠ི~

To hear Alice Keppel talk about her escape from France, one would think she had swum the Channel, with her maid between her teeth.

Mrs Ronnie Greville

~ི༠ི~

It is like a barber's chair that fits all buttocks.

William Shakespeare, All's Well that Ends Well, 1604

The ability of dandelions to tell the time is somewhat exaggerated, owing to the fact that there is always one seed that refuses to be blown off; the time usually turns out to be 37 o'clock.

Miles Kington,
Nature Made Ridiculously Simple, 1983

Long experience has told me that to be criticized is not always to be wrong.

Anthony Eden

Chapter 5

LIFE, DEATH, HEALTH & WEALTH

Before undergoing a surgical operation,
arrange your temporal affairs. You may live.

Ambrose Bierce

We joke because we don't know.

Anon

Whoever said money can't buy happiness didn't
know where to shop.

Gittel Hudnick

*Four fundamentals: life, death, health and wealth, are
normally seen as fairly serious subjects, but are in fact a
surprisingly vast source of amusing irreverence.*

Where there's a will, there are relations.

Michael Gill

I detest life-insurance agents; they always argue that I shall some day die, which is not so.

Stephen Leacock, *Literary Lapses*, 1910

I expect to pass through this world but once and, therefore, if there is anybody that I want to kick in the crutch I had better kick them in the crutch now, for I do not expect to pass this way again.

Maurice Bowra

Death is nature's way of telling you to slow down.

Anon

Eternity is a terrible thought. I mean, where's it going to end?

Tom Stoppard,
Rosencrantz and Guildenstern Are Dead, 1967

In the city a funeral is just an interruption of traffic; in the country it is a form of popular entertainment.

George Ade

If this is dying, I don't think much of it.

Lytton Strachey (on his deathbed)

It's not that I'm afraid to die, I just don't want to be there when it happens.

Woody Allen, *Without Feathers*, 1976

The only thing I regret about my life is the length of it. If I had to live my life again, I'd make all the same mistakes – only sooner.

Tallulah Bankhead

Life would be infinitely happier if we could only be born at the age of eighty and gradually approach eighteen.

Mark Twain

Life is just one damned thing after another.

Elbert Hubbard

I don't want to achieve immortality through my work . . . I want to achieve it through not dying.

Woody Allen

Either this man is dead or my watch has stopped.
Groucho Marx, *A Day at the Races*, 1937

~§~

Death is the most convenient time to tax rich people.
David Lloyd George

~§~

Anyone can get old. All you have to do is live long enough.

Groucho Marx

~§~

I refused to attend his funeral. But I wrote a very nice letter explaining that I approved of it.

Mark Twain

~§~

On the plus side, death is one of the few things that can be done as easily lying down.
Woody Allen, *Getting Even*, 1972

Heaven, as conventionally conceived, is a place so inane, so dull, so useless, so miserable, that nobody has ever ventured to describe a whole day in heaven, though plenty of people have described a day at the seaside.

George Bernard Shaw

Get my "Swan" costume ready!

Anna Pavlova (on her deathbed)

Let us endeavor so to live that when we come to die even the undertaker will be sorry.

Mark Twain

Hovering between wife and death.

James Montgomery

Most people would die sooner than think; in fact, they do.

Bertrand Russell

~ ¿♠. ~

I'm prepared to meet my Maker. Whether my Maker is prepared for the ordeal of meeting me is another matter.

Winston Churchill (in 1949)

~ ¿♠. ~

Millions long for immortality who don't know what to do on a rainy Sunday afternoon.

Susan Ertz

~ ¿♠. ~

If you take epitaphs seriously, we ought to bury the living and resurrect the dead.

Mark Twain

It's a funny old world – a man's lucky if he gets out of it alive.

W.C. Fields, *You're Telling Me*, 1934

～⋅❦⋅～

The meaning of life is that it stops.

Franz Kafka

～⋅❦⋅～

There is no cure for birth or death save to enjoy the interval.

George Santayana

～⋅❦⋅～

Plan for this world as if you expect to live forever; but plan for the hereafter as if you expect to die tomorrow.

Ibn Gabirol

～⋅❦⋅～

Life is something to do when you can't get to sleep.

Fran Lebowitz

The longer I live the more keenly I feel that whatever was good enough for our fathers is not good enough for us.

Oscar Wilde, *The Picture of Dorian Gray*, 1891

Retirement means twice as much husband and half as much money.

Anon

I'm not unwell, I'm fucking dying.

Jeffrey Bernard

Early to rise and early to bed
Makes a man healthy, wealthy and dead.

James Thurber

My doctor is wonderful. Once, when I couldn't afford
an operation, he touched up the X-rays.

Joey Bishop

After two days in hospital, I took a turn for the nurse.

W.C. Fields

And on the label of the stuff,
He wrote this verse;
Which one would think was clear enough,
And terse: –
When taken,
To be well shaken.

George Colman the Younger,
The Newcastle Apothecary, 1797

TB or not TB, that is the congestion.

Woody Allen,
Everything You always Wanted to Know about Sex, 1972

Hungry Joe collected lists of fatal diseases and arranged them in alphabetical order so that he could put his finger without delay on any one he wanted to worry about.

Joseph Heller, *Catch-22*, 1961

I just can't bear to run short of Acetylmethyldimethyloxamidphenylhydrazine.

James Agate (of his asthma medicine)

Smoking is one of the leading causes of statistics.

Fletcher Knebel

I don't need you to remind me of my age, I have a bladder to do that for me.

Stephen Fry, *Paperweight*, 1992

The longer I practise medicine the more convinced I am there are only two types of cases: those that involve taking the trousers off and those that don't.

Alan Bennett, *Habeas Corpus*, 1973

He died of cirrhosis of the liver. It costs money to die of cirrhosis of the liver.

P.G. Wodehouse

You know you're getting old when the candles cost more than the cake.

Bob Hope

You know you're getting old when the candles cost more than the cake.

As a nation we are dedicated to keeping physically fit – and parking as close to the stadium as possible.

Bill Vaughan

Dr Sillitoe's got him on tablets for depression. It's not mental, in fact it's quite widespread. A lot of better-class people get it apparently.

Alan Bennett, *Enjoy*, 1980

Don't knock coronaries. They're all we women have got to guarantee us a prosperous and exciting middle age.

Malcolm Bradbury and Christopher Bigsby,
The After Dinner Game, 1975

If you can't help out with a little money, at least give a sympathetic groan.

Jewish saying

A bank is a place that will lend you money if you can prove that you don't need it.

Bob Hope

Our rabbi is so poor that if he didn't fast every Monday and Thursday, he'd starve to death.

Jewish saying

Saving is a very fine thing. Especially when your parents have done it for you.

Winston Churchill (attrib.)

Money is better than poverty, if only for financial reasons.

Woody Allen, *Without Feathers*, 1972

Economy was always "elegant", and money-spending always "vulgar" and ostentatious – a sort of sour-grapeism, which made us very peaceful and satisfied.

Elizabeth Gaskell, *Cranford*, 1853

There is nothing more demoralizing than a small but adequate income.

Edmund Wilson

One of the strangest things about life is that the poor, who need money the most, are the very ones who never have it.

Finley Dunne

The two most beautiful words in the English language are "cheque enclosed".

Dorothy Parker

When you don't have any money, the problem is food. When you have money, it's sex. When you have both, it's health.

J.P. Donleavy, *The Ginger Man*, 1955

The trouble with being poor is that it takes up all your time.

Willem de Kooning

It's one thing to ask your bank manager for an overdraft to buy 500 begonias for the borders in Haslemere, but quite another to seek financial succour to avail oneself of some of the 5-2 they're offering on Isle de Bourbon for the St Leger.

Jeffrey Bernard

I have long been of the opinion that if work were such a splendid thing the rich would have kept more of it for themselves.

Bruce Grocott

The meek shall inherit the earth, but not the mineral rights.

John Paul Getty

I don't want money. It is only people who pay their
bills who want that, and I never pay mine.
Oscar Wilde, *The Picture of Dorian Gray*, 1891

~•~

Cocaine is God's way of saying you're making too
much money.
Robin Williams

~•~

Economy is going without something you do want in
case you should, some day, want something you
probably won't want.
Anthony Hope, *The Dolly Dialogues*, 1894

~•~

The most pleasing thing that money can buy is
privacy.
Calouste Gulbenkian

We even sell a pair of earrings for under £1, which is cheaper than a prawn sandwich from Marks & Spencers. But I have to say the earrings probably won't last as long.

Gerald Ratner

Whenever I feel the need for exercise I go and lie down for half an hour until the feeling passes.

Will Rogers

Smoking is very bad for you and should only be done because it looks so good. People who don't smoke have a terrible time finding something polite to do with their lips.

P.J. O'Rourke, *Modern Manners*, 1984

We drink each other's health and spoil our own.

Jerome K. Jerome,
Idle Thoughts of an Idle Fellow, 1886

I had examined myself pretty thoroughly and discovered that I was unfit for military service.

Joseph Heller, *Catch-22*, 1961

What's happened to the galloping consumption you had last Thursday? Slowed down to a trot I suppose.

Alan Bennett, *Habeas Corpus*, 1973

He has no more patients because his patients are no more.

Lord Byron (of Dr Polidori)

There is much to be said for the nouveau riche and the Reagans intend to say it all.

Gore Vidal (attrib.)

Come away; poverty's catching.

Aphra Behn, *The Rover*, 1681

Being young is not having any money; being young is not minding not having any money.

Katharine Whitehorn, *Observations*, 1970

Ah'm sorry your Queen has to pay taxes. She's not a wealthy woman.

John Paul Getty (attrib.)

Nobody was ever meant
To remember or invent
What he did with every cent.

Robert Frost

Chapter 6

POLITICS & PHILOSOPHY

If you want to succeed in politics, you must
keep your conscience well under control.

David Lloyd George

A serious and good philosophical work could
be written consisting entirely of jokes.

Ludwig Wittgenstein

*There are many humorous quotations which are not so
much funny as resoundingly true, and rather than
generating gut-wrenching laughter, produce in us a wry
smile. As George Bernard Shaw said: "My way of joking
is to tell the truth."*

All politics are based on the indifference of the majority.

James Reston

Reagan won because he ran against Jimmy Carter. Had Reagan run unopposed, he would have lost.

Mort Sahl

Democracy consists of choosing your dictators, after they've told you what you think it is you want to hear.

Alan Coren

Our ancestors believed in magic, prayers, trickery, browbeating and bullying. I think it would be fair to sum that list up as "Irish politics".

Flann O'Brien, *The Hair of the Dogma*, 1977

A diplomat is a man who thinks twice before he says nothing.

Frederick Sawyer

Politics – the art of getting votes from the poor and campaign funds from the rich by promising to protect each from the other.

Oscar Ameringer

I think it will be a clash between the political will and the administrative won't.

Jonathan Lynn and Anthony Jay,
Yes Prime Minister, 1987

The art of government consists in taking as much money as possible from one class of citizen to give to the other.

Voltaire

Gerry Ford is a nice guy, but he played too much football with his helmet off.

Lyndon B. Johnson

His speeches left the impression of an army of pompous phrases moving over the landscape in search of an idea; sometimes these meandering words would actually capture a straggling thought and bear it triumphantly a prisoner in their midst, until it died of servitude and overwork.

William G. McAdoo (of Warren G. Harding)

Too bad all the people who know how to run the country are busy driving taxicabs and cutting hair.

George Burns

There are three golden rules for parliamentary speakers: "Stand up. Speak up. Shut up".

J.W. Lowther

Better to have him inside the tent pissing out, than outside pissing in.

Lyndon B. Johnson (of J. Edgar Hoover)

A Government that robs Peter to pay Paul can, as a rule, calculate on the support of Paul.

George Bernard Shaw

It has been said that Democracy is the worst form of government except all those other forms that have been tried from time to time.

Winston Churchill

Politicians are the same all over. They promise to build a bridge even when there's no river.

Nikita Khrushchev

Politics: a strife of interests masquerading as a contest of principles.

Ambrose Bierce

The function of socialism is to raise suffering to a higher level.

Norman Mailer

If I were married to her, I'd be sure to have dinner ready when she got home.

George Shultz (of Margaret Thatcher)

There's no trick to being a humorist when you have the whole government working for you.

Will Rogers

I'm convinced there's a small room in the attic of the Foreign Office where future diplomats are taught to stammer.

Peter Ustinov

～❧～

Only a saint could be quite honest in politics, and saints do not enter politics; but Disraeli was as honest as a man can be who is chiefly devoted to his own interests.

Hesketh Pearson

～❧～

When I was a boy I was told that anyone could become President. I'm beginning to believe it.

Clarence Darrow

～❧～

In an autocracy, one person has his way; in an aristocracy a few people have their way; in a democracy no one has his way.

Celia Green, *The Decline and Fall of Science*

I believe in liberalism, but find it hard to believe in liberals.

G.K. Chesterton

The inherent vice of capitalism is the unequal sharing of blessings; the inherent virtue of socialism is the equal sharing of miseries.

Winston Churchill

Avoid all needle drugs – the only dope worth shooting is Richard Nixon.

Abbie Hoffman, *Steal This Book*, 1971

Englishmen never will be slaves; they are free to do whatever the government and public opinion allow them to do.

George Bernard Shaw

Diplomacy is the art of saying "nice doggie" until you can find a rock.

Will Rogers

The honorable gentleman should not generate more indignation than he can conveniently contain.

Winston Churchill

You don't tell deliberate lies, but sometimes you have to be evasive.

Margaret Thatcher

A politician is an animal that can sit on a fence and keep both ears to the ground.

H.L. Mencken

Man is an animal that makes bargains; no other animal does this — no dog exchanges bones with another.

Adam Smith

Democracy means government by discussion, but it is only effective if you can stop people talking.

Clement Attlee

Mr Attlee is a very modest man. But then he has much to be modest about.

Winston Churchill

What's wrong with being a boring kind of guy?

George Bush

The Tory Party is the cream of society – thick and rich and full of clots.

Anon

～ ;♠. ～

I never give the public hell. I just tell the truth and they think it is hell.

Harry S. Truman

～ ;♠. ～

A politician is a man who approaches every question with an open mouth.

George Canning

～ ;♠. ～

Reagan was probably the first modern president to treat the post as a part-time job, one way of helping to fill the otherwise blank days of retirement.

Simon Hoggart, *America*, 1990

Democracy is the theory that the common people know what they want, and deserve to get it good and hard.

H.L. Mencken, *A Book of Burlesques*, 1916

He immatures with age.

Harold Wilson (of Tony Benn)

This island is mainly made of coal and surrounded by fish. Only an organizing genius could produce a shortage of coal and fish at the same time.

Aneurin Bevan

Child: Mama, are Tories born wicked, or do they grow wicked afterwards?
Mother: They're born wicked, and grow worse.

Anon

We know that he has, more than any other man, the gift of compressing the largest amount of words into the smallest amount of thought.

Winston Churchill (of James Ramsay MacDonald)

~ 🝔 ~

It is exciting to have a real crisis on your hands, when you have spent half your political life dealing with humdrum issues like the environment.

Margaret Thatcher

~ 🝔 ~

Democracy is a device that ensures we shall be governed no better than we deserve.

George Bernard Shaw (attrib.)

~ 🝔 ~

Hubert Humphrey talks so fast that listening to him is like trying to read *Playboy* magazine with your wife turning over the pages.

Barry Goldwater

Richard Nixon means never having to say you're sorry.

Wilfred Sheed

He may be a son of a bitch, but he's our son of a bitch.
Franklin D. Roosevelt
(of President Somoza of Nicaragua)

A big cat detained briefly in a poodle parlour, sharpening her claws on the velvet.
Mathew Parris (of Lady Thatcher),
Look Behind You!, 1993

If he ever went to school without any boots it was because he was too big for them.
Ivor Bulmer-Thomas (of Harold Wilson)

Anarchism is a game at which the police can beat you.
George Bernard Shaw, *Misalliance*, 1914

≈⋅≈

Republicans raise dahlias, Dalmatians, and eyebrows.
Democrats raise Airedales, kids and taxes.
Will Stanton

≈⋅≈

There but for the grace of God, goes God.
Winston Churchill (of Stafford Cripps)

≈⋅≈

If he were any dumber, he'd be a tree.
Barry Goldwater
(of Senator William Scott of Virginia)

≈⋅≈

The higher a monkey climbs, the more you see of his ass.
"Vinegar Joe" Stilwell

Is it progress if a cannibal uses a fork?

Stanislaw J. Lec

~ *&* ~

Let us be of good cheer, remembering that the misfortunes hardest to bear are those that never come.

James Russell Lowell

~ *&* ~

Happiness makes up in height what it lacks in length.

Robert Frost

~ *&* ~

It's far easier to forgive an enemy after you've got even with him.

Olin Miller

When a man laughs at his troubles he loses a great many friends. They never forgive the loss of their prerogative.

H.L. Mencken

Intuition is reason in a hurry.

Holbrook Jackson

The follies which a man regrets most in his life are those which he didn't commit when he had the opportunity.

Helen Rowland

The only thing experience teaches us is that experience teaches us nothing.

André Maurois

Consider with yourself what your flattery is worth before you bestow it so freely.

Samuel Johnson

If you keep your mouth shut you will never put your foot in it.

Austin O'Malley

Your arguments against reasoning are so persuasive that one is almost tempted to get down on all fours.

Voltaire (to Rousseau)

The advantage of a bad memory is that one enjoys several times the same good things for the first time.

Friedrich Nietzsche

To sin by silence when they should protest makes cowards of men.

Abraham Lincoln

～🕯～

Even when all the experts agree, they may well be mistaken.

Bertrand Russell

～🕯～

The process of scientific discovery is, in effect, a continual flight from wonder.

Albert Einstein

～🕯～

It is better to waste one's youth than to do nothing with it at all.

Georges Courteline,
La Philosophie de Georges Courteline, 1948

A speaker who does not strike oil in ten minutes should stop boring.

Louis Nizer

~⟨●⟩~

All exact science is dominated by the idea of approximation.

Bertrand Russell

~⟨●⟩~

The trouble with facts is that there are so many of them.

Samuel McChord Crothers

~⟨●⟩~

Nothing will ever be attempted if all possible objections must be first overcome.

Samuel Johnson

I do not believe in the collective wisdom of individual ignorance.

Thomas Carlyle

I think I think; therefore I think I am.

Ambrose Bierce

It is better to have loved and lost than never to have lost at all.

Samuel Butler

Religion is of our own contrivance. What kind of truth is it that it is true on one side of a mountain and false on the other?

Montaigne

Between us, we cover all knowledge; he knows all that can be known, and I know the rest.

Mark Twain (of Rudyard Kipling)

Wise men think their thoughts; fools proclaim them.

Heinrich Heine

I have a simple philosophy: Fill what's empty, empty what's full and scratch where it itches.

Alice Roosevelt Longworth

Man is the only animal that blushes – or ought to.

Mark Twain

We need not worry so much about what man descends from – it's what he descends to that shames the human race.

Mark Twain

A beautiful theory killed by a nasty, ugly little fact.

Thomas Huxley

~ ❦ ~

When dealing with the insane, the best method is to pretend to be sane.

Herman Hesse

~ ❦ ~

I feel that one lies to oneself more than to anyone else.

Lord Byron

~ ❦ ~

If only we'd stop trying to be happy we could have a pretty good time.

Edith Wharton

~ ❦ ~

It is rarely possible to carry the torch of truth through a crowd without singeing somebody's beard.

Joshua Bruyn

Revenge is often like biting a dog because the dog bit you.

Austin O'Malley

The average man's opinions are much less foolish than they would be if he thought for himself.

Bertrand Russell

Heresy is only another word for freedom of thought.

Graham Greene

Everyone complains of his memory, no one of his judgement.

François de La Rochefoucauld

One never dives into the water to save a drowning man more eagerly than when there are others present who dare not take the risk.

Friedrich Nietzsche

~ ❧ ~

Man does not live by words alone, despite the fact that he sometimes has to eat them.

Adlai Stevenson

~ ❧ ~

Man prefers to believe what he prefers to be true.

Francis Bacon

~ ❧ ~

Sin is a dangerous toy in the hands of the virtuous. It should be left to the congenitally sinful, who know when to play with it and when to let it alone.

H.L. Mencken, *The American Mercury*, 1929

Few people can be happy unless they hate some other person, nation, or creed.

Bertrand Russell

~ 🌑 ~

We promise according to our hopes and perform according to our fears.

François de La Rochefoucauld

~ 🌑 ~

True equality exists in the treatment of unequal things unequally.

Aristotle

~ 🌑 ~

The man who is a pessimist before forty-eight knows too much; the man who is an optimist after forty-eight knows too little.

Mark Twain

Happiness is not a goal, it is a by-product.

Eleanor Roosevelt

～❀～

I think that bad philosophers may have a certain influence, good philosophers, never.

Bertrand Russell

～❀～

I have a new philosophy: I'm only going to dread one day at a time.

Charles Schulz

～❀～

Philosophy is common sense in a dress suit.

Oliver Braston

～❀～

Apart from the known and the unknown, what else is there?

Harold Pinter, *The Homecoming*, 1965

What is the conscience but a pair of breeches which while it serves as a cloak both for lewdness and nastiness, may be readily let down in the service of either?

Jonathan Swift

He has not learned the lesson of life who does not every day surmount a fear.

Emerson

Tolerance is only another name for indifference.

W. Somerset Maugham

We act as though comfort and luxury were the chief requirements of life, when all we need to make us really happy is something to be enthusiastic about.

Charles Kingsley

Chapter 7

DEFINITIONS

Psychiatry: the care of the id by the odd.

Anon

Future: that period of time in which our affairs prosper, our friends are true and our happiness is assured.

Ambrose Bierce, *The Devil's Dictionary*, 1911

Technology: the knack of so arranging the world that we need not experience it.

Max Frisch, *Homo Faber*, 1957

Autobiography: an obituary in serial form with the last instalment missing.

Quentin Crisp

Insider Trading: stealing too fast.

Calvin Trillin

Honeymoon: the morning after the knot before.

Anon

Advertising: the rattling of a stick inside a swill bucket.

George Orwell

~⟨●⟩~

Opportunity: a favorable occasion for grasping a disappointment.

Ambrose Bierce, *The Devil's Dictionary*, 1911

~⟨●⟩~

Book: what they make a movie out of for television.

Leonard Louis Levinson

~⟨●⟩~

Cocktail party: a device for paying off obligations to people you don't want to invite to dinner.

Charles Merrill Smith, *Instant Status*, 1972

~⟨●⟩~

A retrospective shudder: a near disaster.

Friedrich Nietzsche

Gossip: hearing something you like about someone you don't.

Earl Wilson

Egotist: a person more interested in himself than in me.

Ambrose Bierce, *The Devil's Dictionary*, 1911

Modesty: the gentle art of enhancing your charm by pretending not to be aware of it.

Edgar Watson Howe,
Ventures in Common Sense, 1919

Editor: one who sorts the wheat from the chaff and prints the chaff.

Adlai Stevenson

Diplomacy: the art of letting somebody else have your way.

David Frost

~•~

Contraceptives: what Protestants use on all conceivable occasions.

Anon

~•~

Baby: a loud noise at one end and no sense of responsibility at the other.

Ronald Knox

~•~

An alcoholic: a man you don't like who drinks as much as you do.

Dylan Thomas

Censor: a man who knows more than he thinks you ought to.

Laurence Peter

~ & ~

Peace: co-existence or no existence.

Bertrand Russell

~ & ~

Gambling: the sure way of getting nothing for something.

Wilson Mizner

~ & ~

Epitaph: an inscription which hopes that virtues acquired by death will have a retroactive effect.

Ambrose Bierce

Journalism: a profession whose business it is to explain to others what it personally does not understand.

Lord Northcliffe

~❧~

Scotsman: a man who, before sending his pyjamas to the laundry, stuffs a sock in each pocket.

Ambrose Bierce

~❧~

Philosophy: unintelligible answers to insoluble problems.

Henry Adams

~❧~

Noise: a stench in the ear. The chief product and authenticating sign of civilization.

Ambrose Bierce, *The Devil's Dictionary*, 1911

Theology: the effort to explain the unknowable in terms of the not worth knowing.

H.L. Mencken

Cynic: a man who, when he smells flowers, looks around for a coffin.

H.L. Mencken

Slander: to lie, or tell the truth, about someone.

Ambrose Bierce

A bore is one who has the power of speech but not the capacity for conversation.

Benjamin Disraeli (attrib.)

Revolution: an abrupt change in the form of misgovernment.

Ambrose Bierce

Experimental psychologist: a scientist who pulls habits out of rats.

Leonard Louis Levinson

~⁑~

Preposition: an enormously versatile part of grammar, as in "What made you pick this book I didn't want to be read to out of up for?"

Winston Churchill

~⁑~

Secret: what we tell everybody to tell nobody.

Ambrose Bierce

~⁑~

Education: the path from cocky ignorance to miserable uncertainty.

Mark Twain

Kleptomaniac: a person who helps himself because he can't help himself.

Henry Morgan

Success is getting what you want, and happiness is wanting what you get.

Dave Gardner

Chapter 8

ANONYMOUS

If it weren't for the optimist, the pessimist
would never know how happy he isn't.

Anon

*It seems that some of the funniest words were said or
written by A. Non. One wonders why he or she never
owned up to them.*

*And as well as off-the-wall humor, this chapter contains
some excellent on-the-wall humor, a selection of graffiti
culled from some of the world's finest lavatories.*

Obscenity is whatever gives a judge an erection.

A gentleman is one who never swears at his wife while ladies are present.

I trust you completely, but please send cash.

Don't get annoyed if your neighbour plays his hi-fi at two o'clock in the morning. Call him at four and tell him how much you enjoyed it.

Does the name Pavlov ring a bell?

Vasectomy means never having to say you're sorry.

Conscience: the thing that feels bad when everything else is feeling good.

A folk-singer is someone who sings through his nose by ear.

You go to a psychiatrist when you're slightly cracked and keep going until you're completely broke.

Pas de deux: father of twins.
Coup de grace: lawnmower.

God gives nuts to those who have no teeth.

He never failed to seek a peaceful solution to a problem when all other possibilities had failed.

~⚬~

They live in a beautiful little apartment overlooking the rent.

~⚬~

All men are of the same mould but some are mouldier than others.

~⚬~

You should make a point of trying every experience once, except incest and folk-dancing.

~⚬~

Nostalgia isn't what it used to be.

~⚬~

Social tact is making your company feel at home, even though you wish they were.

Love may be blind, but jealousy sees too much.

Modesty is the art of encouraging people to find out for themselves how wonderful you are.

A sadist is someone who refuses to be mean to a masochist.

An Irishman is the only man in the world who will step over the bodies of a dozen naked women to get to a bottle of stout.

Memory and teeth grow weaker with time.

The wicked do well in this world, and saints do well in the next.

It is better to have an ugly wife for one's self than a beautiful wife for others.

～ﮗ～

I believe we should all pay our tax bill with a smile. I tried – but they wanted cash.

～ﮗ～

Bigotry is being certain of something you know nothing about.

～ﮗ～

Coitus Interruptus: copulation without population.

～ﮗ～

The difference between genius and stupidity is that genius has its limits.

～ﮗ～

Of course a platonic relationship is possible, but only between husband and wife.

Faith can move mountains, but not furniture.

～·⋅●⋅·～

Middle age is when we can do just as much as ever – but would rather not.

～·⋅●⋅·～

Many know how to flatter but few know how to praise.

～·⋅●⋅·～

When wine goes in, secrets come out.

～·⋅●⋅·～

He's a man who is never lost for a few appropriated words.

～·⋅●⋅·～

A conservative is someone who admires radicals a century after they're dead.

She frowned and called him Mr
Because in sport he kr
And so in spite
That very nite
This Mr kr sr.

No matter what happens, there is someone who knew
it would.

Anonymous critic.
Of the film "I am a Camera": Me no Leica.

A: How's your insomnia?
B: Worse. I can't even sleep when it's time to get up.

Have your eyes ever been checked?
No, Doctor, they've always been blue.

Success is just a matter of luck. Ask any failure.

~·⚫·~

Women tell everybody not to tell anybody.

~·⚫·~

An after-dinner speech should be just like a lady's dress: long enough to cover the subject and short enough to be interesting.

~·⚫·~

My mother made me a homosexual.
If I send her the wool will she make me one?

~·⚫·~

Life is a hereditary disease.

~·⚫·~

Alas, poor yorlik, I knew him backwards.

If Jesus was a Jew, how come he has a Puerto Rican name?

~{●}~

John Wayne is dead.
The hell I am!

~{●}~

Don't open a shop unless you like to smile.

~{●}~

There's no problem so big or complicated that it can't be run away from.

~{●}~

Two in every one people in this country are schizophrenic.

In a "Mens" public lavatory:
I love grils.
The last word was then crossed out and corrected to
"girls", after which someone had added:
What's wrong with us grils?

Chapter 9

~•~

EATING & DRINKING

I always keep a supply of stimulant handy in
case I see a snake – which I also keep handy.
                                        W.C. Fields

*A light-hearted assortment of remarks and puns about
two much-discussed topics.*

Prohibition makes you want to cry into your beer and denies you the beer to cry into.

Don Marquis, *Sun Dial Time*, 1936

Giannini and I were adhering to the two key rules of third world travel:
1. Never run out of whiskey.
2. Never run out of whiskey.

Bill Bryson, *Neither Here Nor There*, 1991

A gentleman never eats. He breakfasts, he lunches, he dines, but he never eats.

Anon

The most sincere love of all is the love of food.

George Bernard Shaw

A psychologist once said that we know little about the conscience except that it is soluble in alcohol.

Thomas Blackburn

If you give him meat no woman in London will be safe.

Mrs Patrick Campbell
(of George Bernard Shaw, a vegetarian)

Love makes the world go round? Not at all. Whisky makes it go round twice as fast.

Compton Mackenzie, *Whisky Galore*, 1947

He that but looketh on a plate of ham and eggs to lust after it, hath already committed breakfast with it in his heart.

C.S. Lewis

I would like to find a stew that will give me heartburn immediately, instead of at three o'clock in the morning.

John Barrymore

~:&:~

Let's get out of these wet clothes and into a dry Martini.

Mae West

~:&:~

After four martinis, my husband turns into a disgusting beast. And after the fifth, I pass out altogether.

Anon

~:&:~

What, when drunk, one sees in other women, one sees in Garbo sober.

Kenneth Tynan, *Curtains*, 1961

I have taken more out of alcohol than alcohol has taken out of me.

Winston Churchill

Sobriety is a real turn-on for me. You can see what you're doing.

Peter O'Toole

Actually, it only takes one drink to get me loaded. Trouble is, I can't remember if it's the thirteenth or fourteenth.

George Burns

I always wake up at the crack of ice.

Joe E. Lewis

No matter what kind of diet you are on, you can usually eat as much as you want of anything you don't like.

Walter Slezak

～⋅🍋⋅～

I brought buckets of caviare and asked all the greediest people I know. They sat in a holy circle and never spoke to me once, except to say, in loud asides, that the others were making pigs of themselves.

Nancy Mitford

～⋅🍋⋅～

My wife is a light eater; as soon as it's light, she starts eating.

Henny Youngman

～⋅🍋⋅～

Sure I eat what I advertise. Sure I eat Wheaties for breakfast. A good bowl of Wheaties with Bourbon can't be beat.

Dizzy Dean, Baseball player

A man shouldn't fool with booze until he's fifty; then he's a damn fool if he doesn't.

William Faulkner

Once, during Prohibition, I was forced to live for days on nothing but food and water.

W.C. Fields

Never drink black coffee at lunch; it will keep you awake in the afternoon.

Jilly Cooper, *How to Survive from Nine to Five*, 1970

Once, during Prohibition, I was forced to live for days on nothing but food and water.

The worst thing about some men is that when they are not drunk they are sober.

William Butler Yeats

The best number for a dinner party is two – myself and a dam' good head waiter.

Nubar Gulbenkian

~°•°~

I will not eat oysters. I want my food dead – not sick, not wounded – dead.

Woody Allen

~°•°~

Clams: I simply cannot imagine why anyone would eat something slimy served in an ashtray.

Miss Piggy, *Miss Piggy's Guide to Life*, 1981

~°•°~

Imprisoned in every fat man a thin one is wildly signalling to be let out.

Cyril Connolly, *The Unquiet Grave*, 1944

If this is coffee, please bring me some tea; but if this is tea, please bring me some coffee.

Abraham Lincoln

I'm on a seafood diet – I see food, I eat it.

Dolly Parton

I've been on a constant diet for the last two decades. I've lost a total of 789 pounds. By all accounts I should be hanging from a charm bracelet.

Erma Bombeck

Artichoke: That vegetable of which one has more at the finish than at the start of a dinner.

Lord Chesterfield

I had no intention of giving her my vital statistics. "Let me put it this way," I said. "According to my girth, I should be a ninety-foot redwood."

Erma Bombeck, *If Life is a Bowl of Cherries, What am I Doing in the Pits?*, 1978

~❧~

One more drink and I'd have been under the host.

Dorothy Parker

~❧~

I'm not so think and you drunk I am.

John Squire

~❧~

A fruit is a vegetable with looks and money. Plus, if you let fruit rot, it turns into wine, something Brussels sprouts never do.

P.J. O'Rourke, *The Bachelor Home Companion*, 1987

I went on a diet, swore off drinking and heavy eating, and in fourteen days I lost two weeks.

Joe E. Lewis

You're not drunk if you can lie on the floor without holding on.

Dean Martin

Chapter 10

HUMAN BEHAVIOR

I've always been interested in people, but I've never liked them.

W. Somerset Maugham

Does human behavior really change that much over time? The following observation was made by Byron over 185 years ago, about a domestic servant abroad:

"The perpetual lamentations after beef and beer, the stupid bigoted contempt for every thing foreign, and insurmountable incapacity of acquiring even a few words of any language, rendered him . . . an encumbrance."

Some speakers electrify their listeners; others only gas them.

Sydney Smith

I hate housework! You make the beds, you do the dishes – and six months later you have to start all over again.

Joan Rivers

Lord Birkenhead is very clever, but sometimes his brains go to his head.

Margot Asquith

I have a face that is a cross between two pounds of halibut and an explosion in an old-clothes closet. If it isn't mobile, it's dead.

David Niven

I had inherited what my father called the art of the advocate, or the irritating habit of looking for the flaw in any argument.

John Mortimer, *Clinging to the Wreckage*, 1982

I met Curzon in Downing Street from whom I got the sort of greeting a corpse would give to an undertaker.

Stanley Baldwin

The trouble with nude dancing is that not everything stops when the music does.

Robert Helpmann

Basic research is what I'm doing when I don't know what I'm doing.

Werner von Braun

Even paranoids have real enemies.

Delmore Schwartz

In Dr Johnson's famous dictionary, patriotism is defined as the last resort of a scoundrel. With all due respect to an enlightened but inferior lexicographer, I beg to submit that it is the first.

Ambrose Bierce

If I have ever made any valuable discoveries, it has been owing more to patient attention than to any other talent.

Isaac Newton

He's turned his life round. He used to be depressed and miserable. Now he's miserable and depressed.

David Frost

One disadvantage of being a hog is that at any moment some blundering fool may try to make a silk purse out of your wife's ear.

J.B. Morton, *By the Way*, 1931

I do not see why I should break my neck because a dog chooses to run after a nasty smell.

Arthur James Balfour
(when asked why he did not like to hunt)

Thank heavens the sun has gone in, and I don't have to go out and enjoy it.

Logan Pearsall Smith, *Afterthoughts*, 1931

All the same, sir, I would put some of the colonies in your wife's name.

Joseph Herman Hertz
(to George VI during World War II)

To do each day two things one dislikes is a precept I have followed scrupulously: every day I have got up and I have gone to bed.

W. Somerset Maugham

Some people pay a compliment as if they expected a receipt.

Frank McKinney Hubbard

People who live in glass houses have to answer the bell.

Bruce Patterson

If an elderly but distinguished scientist says that something is possible he is almost certainly right, but if he says that it is impossible, he is very probably wrong.

Arthur C. Clarke

Faith, to my mind, is a stiffening process, a sort of mental starch, which ought to be applied as sparingly as possible.

E.M. Forster, *Two Cheers for Democracy*, 1951

I remember the average curate at home as something between a eunuch and a snigger.

Ronald Firbank, *The Flower Beneath the Foot*, 1923

An atheist is a man who has no invisible means of support.

John Buchan

Don't get smart alecksy
With the galaxy
Leave the atom alone.

E.Y. Harburg

You're always a little disappointing in person because you can't be the edited essence of yourself.

Mel Brooks

Fortunately, just as things were blackest, the war broke out.

Joseph Heller, *Catch-22*, 1961

(To Groucho Marx): Is that your real name?
Marx: No, I'm breaking it in for a friend.

His face shining like Moses, his teeth like the Ten Commandments, all broken.

Herbert Beerbohm Tree (of Israel Zangwill)

My reputation's terrible, which comforts me a lot.

Noël Coward

Most of my friends seem to be either dead, extremely deaf or living on the wrong side of Kent.

John Gielgud

Somebody's boring me, I think it's me.

Dylan Thomas

Whenever a friend succeeds, a little something in me dies.

Gore Vidal

I can resist everything except temptation.

Oscar Wilde

I am not the type who wants to go back to the land; I am the type who wants to go back to the hotel.

Fran Lebowitz, *Social Studies*, 1981

I am extraordinarily patient, provided I get my own way in the end.

Margaret Thatcher

～ ୧ ～

I became one of the stately homos of England.

Quentin Crisp, *The Naked Civil Servant*, 1968

～ ୧ ～

When I'm good I'm very, very good, but when I'm bad, I'm better.

Mae West

～ ୧ ～

The rush-hour traffic I'd just as soon miss
When caraftercarismovinglikethis.

Robert Lauher

I don't want any yes-men around me. I want everybody to tell me the truth even if it costs them their jobs!

Sam Goldwyn

He's very, very well known. I'd say he's world-famous in Melbourne.

Dame Edna Everage

To me, old age is always fifteen years older than I am.

Bernard Baruch

One green bottle
Drop it in the bank . . .
Heaps of bottles
And yesterday's a blank
But we'll save the planet,
Tinkle, tinkle, clank!

Wendy Cope, *A Green Song*, 1992

I have noticed that the people who are late are often so much jollier than the people who have to wait for them.

E.V. Lucas, *365 Days and One More*, 1926

To Americans, English manners are far more frightening than none at all.

Randall Jarrell

Actually, there is no way of making vomiting courteous. You have to do the next best thing, which is to vomit in such a way that the story you tell about it later will be amusing.

P.J. O'Rourke, *Modern Manners*, 1984

Punctuality is the virtue of the bored.

Evelyn Waugh

I regard you with an indifference closely bordering on aversion.

  Robert Louis Stevenson, *New Arabian Nights*, 1882

I like long walks, especially when they are taken by people who annoy me.

Fred Allen

JUDGE: You are extremely offensive, young man.
SMITH: As a matter of fact, we both are, and the only difference between us is that I am trying to be, and you can't help it.

F.E. Smith, Earl of Birkenhead, 1933

If the desire to kill and the opportunity to kill came always together, who would escape hanging?

Mark Twain

I've just learned about his illness; let's hope it's nothing trivial.

Irvin Cobb

Forgive your enemies but never forget their names.

John F. Kennedy

What time he can spare from the adornment of his person he devotes to the neglect of his duties.

William Hepworth Thompson (of Richard Jebb), *With Dearest Love to All*, 1960

My father was a Creole, his father a Negro, and his father a monkey; my family, it seems, begins where yours left off.

Alexandre Dumas (Père)

When a man tells me he's going to put all his cards on the table, I always look up his sleeve.

Lord Hore-Belisha

Braddock: Winston, you're drunk.
Churchill: Bessie, you're ugly. But tomorrow I shall be sober.

Winston Churchill (to Labour MP Bessie Braddock)

I thoroughly disapprove of duels. If a man should challenge me, I would take him kindly and forgivingly by the hand and lead him to a quiet place and kill him.

Mark Twain

The Falkland's Incident was a quarrel between two bald men over a comb.

Jorge Luis Borges

A population explosion is something that happens when people take leave of their census.

Anon

The human brain starts working the moment you are born and never stops until you stand up to speak in public.

Sir George Jessel

Every Tom Dick and Harry is called Arthur.

Sam Goldwyn

Speaking of Eleanor Roosevelt: No woman has so comforted the distressed or so distressed the comfortable.

Clare Boothe Luce

I don't pay any attention to him. I don't even ignore him.

Sam Goldwyn

≈ ⁑ ≈

I will not go down to posterity talking bad grammar.

Benjamin Disraeli

≈ ⁑ ≈

His huff arrived and he departed in it.

Alexander Woollcott

≈ ⁑ ≈

The greatest thing since they reinvented unsliced bread.

William Keagan

≈ ⁑ ≈

No matter. The dead bird does not leave the nest.

Winston Churchill
(on being told that his fly was undone)

Any man who hates dogs and babies can't be all bad.

Leo Rosten (of W.C. Fields)

I am a deeply superficial person.

Andy Warhol

Success didn't spoil me; I've always been insufferable.

Fran Lebowitz

Don't you realize that missionaries are the divinely provided food for destitute and underfed cannibals? Whenever they are on the brink of starvation, Heaven in its infinite mercy sends them a nice plump missionary.

Oscar Wilde

Laughter is the sensation of feeling good all over, and showing it principally in one spot.

Josh Billings,
The Complete Works of Josh Billings, 1919

~•~

The brain is a wonderful organ; it starts working the moment you get up in the morning and does not stop until you get into the office.

Robert Frost

~•~

When you look like your passport photo, it's time to go home.

Erma Bombeck (attrib.)

~•~

I always thought that once you grew up you could do anything you wanted – stay up all night or eat ice-cream straight out of the container.

Bill Bryson

Perfume is a subject dear to my heart. I have so many favourites: Arome de Grenouille, Okéfénôkée, Eau Contraire, Fume de ma Tante, Blast du Past, Kèrmes, Je Suis Swell, and Attention S'il Vous Plaît, to name but a few.

Miss Piggy, *Miss Piggy's Guide to Life*, 1981

Anybody who goes to see a psychiatrist ought to have his head examined.

Sam Goldwyn

It usually takes me more than three weeks to prepare a good impromptu speech.

Mark Twain

Pot is like a gang of Mexican bandits in your brain. They wait for thoughts to come down the road, then tie them up and trash them.

Kevin Rooney

What's on your mind? – if you'll forgive the over-statement.

Fred Allen

~:&.~

McEnroe . . . did his complete Krakatoa number.

Clive James

~:&.~

When choosing between two evils, I always like to take the one I've never tried before.

Mae West

~:&.~

The General was essentially a man of peace, except in his domestic life.

Oscar Wilde, *The Importance of Being Earnest*, 1895

~:&.~

On opening a new annexe at Vancouver City Hall: I declare this thing open – whatever it is.

Prince Philip, Duke of Edinburgh

I have been in a youth hostel . . . You are put in a kitchen with seventeen venture scouts with behavioural difficulties and made to wash swedes.

Victoria Wood,
Mens Sana in Thingummy Doodah, 1990

Drugs have taught an entire generation of American kids the metric system

P.J. O'Rourke, *Modern Manners*, 1984

Met a guy this morning with a glass eye. He didn't tell me – it just came out in the conversation.

Jerry Dennis

He had but one eye, and the popular prejudice runs in favour of two.

Charles Dickens, *Nicholas Nickleby*, 1839

What is my loftiest ambition? I've always wanted to throw an egg into an electric fan.

Oliver Herford

~🔔~

Commuter – one who spends his life
In riding to and from his wife;
A man who shaves and takes a train,
And then rides back to shave again.

E.B. White

~🔔~

There is a school of thought that believes that sleep is for the night. You seem to be out to disprove them.

Alan Ayckbourn, *Woman in Mind*, 1986

~🔔~

I do not object to people looking at their watches when I am speaking. But I strongly object when they start shaking them to make certain they are still going.

Lord Birkett

There is no arguing with Johnson, for when his pistol misses fire, he knocks you down with the butt end of it.

Oliver Goldsmith (of Samuel Johnson)

A snappish OAP with a temper like an arthritic corgi.

Jean Rook (of Prince Philip)

Of course I don't want to go to a cocktail party . . . If I wanted to stand around with a load of people I don't know eating bits of cold toast I can get caught shoplifting and go to Holloway.

Victoria Wood,
Mens Sana in Thingummy Doodah, 1990

I had a monumental idea this morning, but I didn't like it.

Sam Goldwyn

Adam and Eve had many advantages, but the principal one was that they escaped teething.

Mark Twain

≈·{●·≈

In my day, the principal concerns of university students were sex, smoking dope, rioting and learning. Learning was something you did only when the first three weren't available.

Bill Bryson, *The Lost Continent*, 1989

≈·{●·≈

Stand firm in your refusal to remain conscious during algebra. In real life, I assure you, there is no such thing as algebra.

Fran Lebowitz, *Social Studies*, 1981

≈·{●·≈

Universities are full of knowledge; the freshmen bring a little in and the seniors take none away, so knowledge accumulates.

Abbott Lawrence Lowell

In examinations, those who do not wish to know ask questions of those who cannot tell.

Walter Raleigh, *Laughter from a Cloud*, 1923

I know I've got a degree. Why does that mean I have to spend my life with intellectuals? I've got a life-saving certificate but I don't spend my evenings diving for a rubber brick with my pyjamas on.

Victoria Wood,
Mens Sana in Thingummy Doodah, 1990

If you think that education is expensive, try ignorance.

Derek Bok

To the man-in-the-street, who, I'm sorry to say,
Is a keen observer of life,
The word "Intellectual" suggests straight away
A man who's untrue to his wife.

W.H. Auden

For every person who wants to teach, there are approximately thirty who don't want to learn – much.
W.C. Sellar and R.J. Yeatman,
And Now All This, 1932

~ ❦ ~

I have nothing to declare except my genius.
Oscar Wilde

~ ❦ ~

Underneath this flabby exterior is an enormous lack of character.
Oscar Levant, *Memoirs of an Amnesiac*, 1965

~ ❦ ~

The English are not happy unless they are miserable,
The Irish are not at peace unless they are at war,
The Scots are not at home unless they are abroad.
George Orwell

I don't like Norwegians at all. The sun never sets, the bar never opens, and the whole country smells of kippers.

Evelyn Waugh

Hollywood is the only place you can wake up in the morning and hear the birds coughing in the trees.

Joe Frisco (attrib.)

She said that all the sights in Rome were called after London cinemas.

Nancy Mitford, *Pigeon Pie*, 1940

The Pacific Ocean was a body of water surrounded on all sides by elephantiasis and other dread diseases.

Joseph Heller, *Catch-22*, 1961

Holland: Apart from cheese and tulips, the main product of the country is advocaat, a drink made from lawyers.

Alan Coren, *The Sanity Inspector*, 1974

In England people actually try to be brilliant at breakfast. That is so dreadful of them! Only dull people are brilliant at breakfast.

Oscar Wilde, *An Ideal Husband*, 1895

German is the most extravagantly ugly language. It sounds like someone using a sick-bag on a 747.

William Rushton, *Holiday Inn, Ghent*, 1984

Why should I travel when I am already here?
(A Venetian's response to being asked why he did not travel.)

Anon

The English instinctively admire any man who has no talent and is modest about it.

James Agee

Fleet Street has a very animated appearance; but I think the full tide of human existence is at Charing Cross.

Samuel Johnson

Waiting for the German verb is surely the ultimate thrill.

Flann O'Brien, *The Hair of the Dogma*, 1977

The English: cold-blooded queers with nasty complexions and terrible teeth who once conquered half the world but still haven't figured out central heating. They warm their beers and chill their baths and boil all their food, including bread.

P.J. O'Rourke

Worth seeing, yes; but not worth going to see.

> Samuel Johnson (of the Giant's Causeway)

~☙~

If one could only teach the English how to talk, and the Irish how to listen, society here would be quite civilized.

> Oscar Wilde, *An Ideal Husband*, 1895

~☙~

There are few more impressive sights than a Scotsman on the make.

> J.M. Barrie, *What Every Woman Knows*, 1908

~☙~

My first rule of travel is never to go to a place that sounds like a medical condition and Critz clearly was an incurable disease involving flaking skin.

> Bill Bryson, *The Lost Continent*, 1989

My one claim to originality among Irishmen is that I never made a speech.

George More, *Ave*, 1911

From Poland to polo in one generation.

Arthur Caesar (of Darryl Zanuck)

Let's be frank, the Italians' technological contribution to humankind stopped with the pizza oven.

Bill Bryson, *Neither Here Nor There*, 1991

They say travel broadens the mind; but you must have the mind.

G.K. Chesterton, *The Shadow of the Shark*, 1921

It is unthinkable for a Frenchman to arrive at middle age without having syphilis and the Croix de la Légion d'honneur.

André Gide

The most dangerous thing is to make a friend of an Englishman, because he'll come sleep in your closet rather than spend ten shillings on a hotel.

Truman Capote

In America there are two classes of travel – first class, and with children.

Robert Benchley, *Pluck and Luck*, 1925

Hollywood: where people from Iowa mistake each other for movie stars.

Fred Allen

I don't like men who live, by choice, out of their own country. I don't like interior decorators. I don't like Germans. I don't like buggers and I don't like Christian Scientists.

Duff Cooper

The people of Crete unfortunately make more history than they can consume locally.

Saki, *Chronicles of Clovis*, 1911

If there were any of Australia's original inhabitants living in Melbourne they were kept well out of the way of nice people; unless, of course, they could sing.

Barry Humphries, *More Please*, 1992

I cannot forecast to you the action of Russia. It is a riddle wrapped up in a mystery inside an enigma.

Winston Churchill (in 1939)

A big hard-boiled city with no more personality than a paper cup.

Raymond Chandler, *The Little Sister*, 1949

Hollywood: A place where they shoot too many pictures and not enough actors.

Walter Winchell

Saigon is like all the other great modern cities of the world. It's the mess left over from people getting rich.

P.J. O'Rourke, *Give War a Chance*, 1992

What is better than presence of mind in a railway accident?
Absence of body.

Punch

Pat: He was an Anglo-Irishman.
Meg: In the blessed name of God what's that?
Pat: A Protestant with a horse.

Brendan Behan, Hostage, 1958

You can always reason with a German. You can always reason with a barnyard animal, too, for all the good it does.

P.J. O'Rourke, Holidays in Hell, 1988

Poor Mexico, so far from God and so near to the United States.

Porfirio Diaz

California is a fine place to live – if you happen to be an orange.

Fred Allen

France is the only country where the money falls apart and you can't tear the toilet paper.

Billy Wilder

The English find ill-health not only interesting but respectable and often experience death in the effort to avoid making a fuss.

Pamela Frankau, *Pen to Paper*, 1961

The English country gentleman galloping after a fox – the unspeakable in full pursuit of the uneatable.

Oscar Wilde

In Boston they ask: "How much does he know?" In New York: "How much is he worth?" In Philadelphia: "Who were his parents?"

Mark Twain

In Italy for thirty years under the Borgias, they had warfare, terror, murder, bloodshed. They produced Michelangelo, Leonardo da Vinci and the Renaissance. In Switzerland they had brotherly love, five hundred years of democracy and peace, and what did they produce – the cuckoo clock!

Orson Welles to Joseph Cotton,
The Third Man, 1949

What I learned by being in France was learning to be better satisfied with my own country.

Samuel Johnson

England is the most class-ridden country under the sun. It is a land of snobbery and privilege, ruled largely by the old and silly.

George Orwell, *The Lion and the Unicorn*, 1941

When in Turkey, do as the turkeys do.

Honore de Balzac

The only nation I've ever been tempted to feel really racist about are the Swiss – a whole country of phobic handwashers living in a giant Barclays Bank.

Jonathan Raban,
Arabia Through the Looking Glass, 1979

The best thing that can be said for Norwegian television is that it gives you the sensation of a coma without the worry and inconvenience.

Bill Bryson, *Neither Here Nor There*, 1991

The French will only be united under the threat of danger. Nobody can simply bring together a country that has 265 kinds of cheese.

Charles de Gaulle

I could come back to America . . . to die . . . but never, never to live.

Henry James

~❧~

Those bellhops in Miami are tip-happy. I ordered a deck of playing cards and the bellboy made fifty-two trips to my room.

Henny Youngman

~❧~

The Texan turned out to be good-natured, generous and likable. In three days no one could stand him.

Joseph Heller, *Catch-22*, 1961

~❧~

Never criticize Americans. They have the best taste that money can buy.

Miles Kington

I landed at Orly airport and discovered my luggage wasn't on the same plane. My bags were finally traced to Israel where they were opened and all my trousers were altered.

Woody Allen

There is nothing wrong with Southern California that a rise in the ocean level wouldn't cure.

Ross MacDonald

Americans are broad-minded people. They'll accept the fact that a person can be an alcoholic, a dope fiend, a wife beater, and even a newspaperman, but if a man doesn't drive there's something wrong with him.

Art Buchwald

We have passed a lot of water since then.

Sam Goldwyn (attrib.)

Chapter 11

SPORT & LEISURE

No one is more sensitive about his game than a
weekend tennis player.

Jimmy Cannon

Boxing's all about getting the job done as
quickly as possible – whether it takes ten or
fifteen or twenty rounds.

Frank Bruno

*A medley of entertaining quotations from the field of sport
as well as some howlers made by TV and radio
commentators, disc jockeys and politicians: the things they
wish they'd never said.*

A fishing rod is a stick with a hook at one end and a fool at the other.

Samuel Johnson

～⋅𝕝⋅～

He loved to walk sideways towards them, like a grimly playful crab.

R.C. Robertson-Glasgow (of George Gunn),
Cricket Prints, 1943

～⋅𝕝⋅～

We didn't underestimate them. They were a lot better than we thought.

Bobby Robson (of Camaroon)

～⋅𝕝⋅～

The least thing upset him on the links. He missed short putts because of the uproar of the butterflies in the adjoining meadows.

P.G. Wodehouse, *The Clicking of Cuthbert*, 1922

That man can't sing – he's the only nigger in the world ain't got rhythm.

Muhammad Ali (of Joe Frazier)

If you want to take long walks, take long walks. If you want to hit things with a stick, hit things with a stick. But there's no excuse for combining the two and putting the results on TV.

National Lampoon, 1979

Years ago we discovered the exact point, the dead centre of middle age. It occurs when you are too young to take up golf and too old to rush up to the net.

Franklin P. Adams, *Nods and Becks*, 1944

Another good reducing exercise consists in placing both hands against the table edge and pushing back.

Robert Quillen

Some people think football is a matter of life and death . . . I can assure them it is much more serious than that.

Bill Shankly

Golf is a good walk spoiled.

Mark Twain

The sport of ski-ing consists of wearing three thousand dollars' worth of clothes and equipment and driving two hundred miles in the snow in order to stand around at a bar and get drunk.

P.J. O'Rourke, *Modern Manners*, 1984

Like a Volvo, Borg is rugged, has good after-sales service and is very dull.

Clive James

The trouble with referees is that they just don't care which side wins.

Tom Canterbury

Nick Faldo has shown himself to be a worthy world number one by finishing second here today.

Golf commentator

Ten Tour de France riders crashed, two retired after falls, another dropped out when diarrhoea slowed him to the point of elimination . . .

James Richardson

He's a very dangerous bowler – innocuous, if you like.

David Lloyd

The Gullikson twins here. An interesting pair — both from Wisconsin.

Dan Maskell

∽⟨🔔⟩∽

These ball boys are marvellous. You don't even notice them. There's a left-handed one over there. I noticed him earlier.

Max Robertson

∽⟨🔔⟩∽

It's quite clear that Virginia Wade is thriving on the pressure now that the pressure on her to do well is off.

Harry Carpenter

∽⟨🔔⟩∽

And the line-up for the final of the Women's 400 metres hurdles includes three Russians, two East Germans, a Pole, a Swede and a Frenchman.

David Coleman

And the mile once again becomes the focal point where it's always been.

Ron Pickering

It's not only a race against the clock but a race against time itself.

Presenter, BBC Wales

This is their first single, and their most successful so far.

Mark Curry

Ron White was not one of the very first original members of the Motown staff, but eventually he was.

Smokey Robinson

We all live in the twentieth century. Well, I don't live in the twentieth century.

Dan Quayle

～•～

The British public sees with blinding clarity.

Michael Heseltine

～•～

Jim Reeves died on 31st July 1964, but his career was not affected by his death.

Ed Stewart

～•～

Teenage orphans are to be given a say in their future. Health Secretary Virginia Bottomley has announced new legislation which will allow them to stay in touch with their natural parents.

Sky News

Anybody in their right mind who doesn't ask you needs his head examined.

Sean Rafferty

As I said before and I said yesterday, this is one of the key questions that will be decided or not decided at Edinburgh.

Douglas Hurd

I'm for a stronger death penalty.

President George Bush

I can definitely say, that had the police not been there this morning, there would have been no arrests.

Arthur Scargill